Preparing for Revival

Michael Angley Ogwuche

Dear Angel,
I hope you will enjoy reading this Book as much as I did in writing it.

Michael
18/03/21

O&U
Onwards & Upwards

Onwards and Upwards Publishers

4 The Old Smithy, London Road, Rockbeare,
Exeter, EX5 2EA, United Kingdom.
www.onwardsandupwards.org

First edition, published in the United Kingdom by Onwards and Upwards Publishers (2020).

ISBN: 978-1-78815-529-8
Typeface: Sabon LT
Graphic design: LM Graphic Design

About the Author

The Revd Michael Angley Ogwuche began to preach the gospel in 1987 shortly after he accepted Jesus Christ in the city of Kaduna, Nigeria where he was born. He believes we are a broken people living in a broken world and needing a Saviour to save us from our broken lives; thus, he considers the Bible an indispensable and critical tool for the navigation of our world.

Michael has served in the roles of street evangelist, Director of Bible Correspondence, associate pastor and more recently as National Chaplaincy Coordinator of the Church of God Scotland. Presently Michael serves as an R&R presbyter with the Methodist Church of Britain at the Southport Circuit where he resides with his family and has pastoral oversight of three churches. In addition, he hosts the *Pneuma Podcast* on various Internet platforms including iTunes, publishes a quarterly personal newsletter, *The Adventure,* and is a member of the Association of Christian Writers.

Michael holds a Bachelor of Arts and a Postgraduate Diploma in Theology with focus on Global Mission and Culture. He is passionate about social justice and above all a reasonable enthusiast for Jesus Christ in a post-truth world.

Endorsements

One of the current shifts in world Christianity and world mission is that we now have reverse missionaries from Africa, Asia and Latin America in the UK. The Christianity that is being proclaimed by Global South reverse missionaries and pastors is conservative and reminds of Biblical Christianity. Michael Ogwuche is one of those reverse missionaries and through this book he reminds us the basic tenets of Christianity [necessary to] experience revival. I would recommend this book to those who wants to understand the passion of African reverse missionaries in the UK and for those who want to experience revival in their lives!

Rev. Israel Oluwole Olofinjana
Pastor, Woolwich Central Baptist Church, London
Director, Centre for Missionaries from the Majority World

In *Preparing for Revival,* the author makes clear and compelling his burning desire to get lives transformed and God glorified, explaining how it all starts with "return[ing] to God's word and His ways". Written in an engaging style that engenders contemplative action, Revd Michael Angley Ogwuche instructively places demand on his readers, inviting them at times to do life-changing and enriching things like "ask[ing] the Holy Spirit to come into your heart and dwell in you". ... Revival only happens in partnership with God, and it needs preparedness. It is never experienced independent of God, and is never a happenstance. Revd Ogwuche wants everyone to know and apply that – and carefully provides Bible-based 'how-to' in this book.

Rev. C. Paschal Eze
Vice President for Communications and Spiritual Life
Detroit Rescue Mission Ministries (DRMM), Detroit, Michigan, USA

Preparing for Revival by Michael Ogwuche contains both deep despair and great hope. He shares his deep concern for the state of the church and our nation, and the potential for revival. He writes of the gradual moving away from God and His ways, and calls us to a closer relationship with God, which includes deep repentance of our own sin (detoxing our souls), the sin of the church and the sin of the nation. This book is rooted in both the Old and New Testaments, in the work of God the Triune God and in our relationship with Father, Jesus, Holy Spirit. He indicates how the story of Nehemiah encourages us to rebuild through seeking God afresh in prayer and fasting, grieving over the state of the church and nation, and rebuilding together. It is not just theory, it is also practical, and includes prayers of repentance and renewal. Through renewing our covenant relationship with God, we can experience God's merciful blessings afresh.

Revd Derek Balsdon
Development Worker
Methodist Evangelicals Together

Preparing for Revival echoes this generation's voice of one crying out in the wilderness. It is a gift that God is giving to the European church today. As an African minister in Britain, Reverend Ogwuche makes maximum use of his critical distance from British culture to help us hear what the Spirit is saying to the church in Britain and discern how to evangelise among all those living here today. If you loved Leonard Ravenhill, you will love this book.

Dr Harvey C. Kwiyani
Programme Leader, MA African Christianity
Liverpool Hope University, Liverpool

The need of the 21st century church is spiritual growth, which forms the catalyst for reawakening and a genuine lasting revival. This book, *Preparing for Revival*, is geared towards meeting that need, hence I consider it a tool for evangelism. It is in fact a catechism for Evangelical Christianity. A pastoral companion and a textbook for bible college. It is a must read for every new convert in the Christian faith.

The Right Revd Dr E. Dennis Ejila
Presiding Bishop of King Jesus Ministries
The Gambia, West Africa

Acknowledgements

No adventure can be complete without resources and so it is with this project. The task of completing this book would not have been possible without help from all quarters as I have been influenced by all.

My appreciation goes to Christiana, my wife and ministry help for so many years, for her support throughout.

To the editors and proof-readers of this book.

To Cliff College, Calver Hope Valley, and the Nazarene Theological College, Manchester, England; these two institutions of high repute impacted in me the ability to think constructively without losing my faith in Jesus Christ.

To Bishop Dennis Tanner of The Church of God Scotland, a man full of grace who gave me the opportunity to serve in Scotland.

I thank the Southport Methodist Circuit, especially those at my three congregations – Leyland Road, Russell Road and Victoria Methodist Churches. These people gave me the space to minister the undiluted Word of God each time.

I will not forget Mr Frank Woods, Mrs Moira Chadwick, Mrs Andrea Fitzpatrick and Mrs Debs Attwater, Mr & Mrs David Potts, and Mrs Jean McKenna, for their encouragements and prayers.

To my children, Shalom, BrookCherith and Favour for being there.

To my three sisters, Christiana, Margaret and Patricia, for their tireless efforts in praying for me.

My thanks go to all those who have supported me directly or indirectly and to fellow labourers in God's vineyard.

My gratitude is to Jesus Christ who called an unworthy person like me into His marvellous light.

Finally, I am grateful in advance to you who are reading this; without you this book would be useless.

To Sienna, Favour,
BrookCherith and Shalom

Acknowledgements

Contents

Preface

"How long will you falter between two opinions?"

1 Kings 18:21

To put the content of this book in perspective it is important that readers understand the context from which it is written. Originally from Nigeria, I had been working in The Gambia as an associate pastor prior to moving to Britain. My knowledge of the United Kingdom, the land of kings and queens, churches, castles and more importantly colonial masters, was gathered from books and my dad's stories about his experience serving with the British Army in Myanmar (formerly Burma), his brief visit to England, and subsequently serving the colonial District Officer in our home town of Otukpo, in present day Benue State, Nigeria, as his personal cook.

In August 2001 opportunity presented itself through the International Scripture Union to represent The Gambia in their conference which was held at the University of Nottingham. My preconceived idea was that I was going to a 'Christian Country' – and yes, I met many Christians at the conference – but the story was different when I finally got the chance to see what British society is really like. Not long after the conference I was graciously admitted into Cliff College, where I started to study for a Bachelor's degree in Theology, during which time I had the privilege to go on mission trips to many parts of the country; these afforded me a critical insight into the spiritual state of the nation.

One of these mission trips was to Connah's Quay, Flintshire. On our return to Cliff College, in Calver Hope Valley, the view from our car window showed dry and browning vegetation delicately pitched in the majestic Peak District area of England. (It had not been raining for some time that autumn.) My thoughts drifted to the time of the famine that God had sent to Israel for her apostasy in turning away from their God and for building altars to the Canaanite 'god' Baal. God had sent Elijah to curse the land with famine as a sign of His judgment and to bring His people back to Him.

The reality of our spiritual condition is something that has been troubling me deeply since my arrival to the United Kingdom; this sense of dryness and the discernible spiritual famine make me feel literally helpless. This, of course, is not just limited to the United Kingdom; it is happening across the world. However, whilst most of the Global South, especially Africa and Asia, struggles under the weight of a syncretic gospel, the Global North contends with a liberal gospel. The latter appears to be more powerful than the former as a result of the power of socio-cultural engineering, an apparent consequence of the postmodern age, and more recently of post-truth, valuing reason and rationality above faith and morality. Believing that our society is evolving towards perfection, we have rejected the God of the Bible and the simplicity of the gospel message. We have set up other gods according to the dictates of our own conscience and our scientific minds. We say that a form of 'godliness' exists in our society because of our civil institutions, but it is a godliness deprived of power. We have erected our own altars to Baal, allowing the entry of lawlessness and perversion of every kind. I dare say that like the prophet Elijah of old, we too are in a famine situation without realising it; but the effects – moral confusion and dryness – are seen everywhere.

Considering the above, I am strongly reminded of the reflection of Dr Edward Wilmot Blyden (1832-1912). He pointed out:

> *Africa may yet prove to be the spiritual conservatory of the world ... when the civilized nations, in consequence of their wonderful material development, shall have had their spiritual perceptions darkened and their spiritual susceptibilities blunted through the agency of captivating and absorbing materialism, it may be that they may have to resort to Africa to recover the simple elements of faith.*[1]

While the above statement may be open to debate, as part of the African diaspora I can see an element of truth in these words, given the amount of involvement of Africans in mission in the civilized nations today. Like many other African missionaries in the Global North, I have huge interest in global mission and culture and therefore seriously consider myself a 'reverse missionary', which describes a situation where

---

[1] Robert W. July, The Origins of Modern African Thought: Its development in West Africa during the ninetieth and twentieth centuries (Trenton: Africa World Press, 2004), 219.

missionaries from former mission fields engage in mission in territories that previously sent out the missionaries.

The proliferation of Christian missionary activities out of Africa and other countries of the Global South are undeniably some of the leading global evangelistic movements today. In Europe, for example, African Initiated Churches (AICs) or African Diaspora Churches have been at the vanguard of the exceptional growth now christened as 'Reverse and Diaspora Mission' which clearly challenges the traditional concept of mission as practised by mission agencies in the past and perhaps still being practised.

Let me return to the famine in Elijah's day so that my message becomes plain to all. After three years of famine in Israel, which was so severe the crops had dried up and the livestock were dying, Elijah was sent to Ahab, king of Israel. Ahab was the husband of Jezebel who had introduced Baal worship. Elijah instructed Ahab to gather at Mount Carmel the four hundred and fifty prophets of Baal and the four hundred prophets of Asherah who served Jezebel.[2]

When all the prophets together with the children of Israel were gathered, Elijah challenged the people thus:

"How long will you falter between two opinions? If the LORD is God, follow Him; but if Baal, follow him." But the people answered him not a word.

1 Kings 18:21

Then Elijah ordered two bulls to be presented, one for the prophets and one for himself; each bull was to be cut in pieces, laid on the wood, but without any fire under it. Then the prophets would call on the name of their gods, and he would call on the name of the LORD: "...and the God who answers by fire, He is God."

So the prophets of Baal prepared the altar and the bull and called on the name of Baal from morning till noon, saying, "O Baal, hear us!" But no one answered. Then they leaped about the altar; they cried aloud, and cut themselves, as was their custom, with knives and lances, until the blood gushed out on them. They even prophesied until the time of the evening sacrifice.[3]

---

[2] See 1 Kings 18:1-45
[3] See 1 Kings 18:26-29

But there was no voice; no one answered, no one paid attention.

1 Kings 18:29

Now it was Elijah's turn.

Then Elijah said to all the people, "<u>Come near</u> to me." So all the people came near to him. And he <u>repaired</u> the altar of the LORD that was broken down. And Elijah took <u>twelve stones</u>, according to the number of the tribes of the sons of Jacob, to whom the word of the LORD had come, saying, "Israel shall be your name." Then with the stones he built an altar in the name of the LORD; and he made a trench around the altar large enough to hold two seahs of seed. And he put the wood in order, cut the bull in pieces, and laid it on the wood, and said, "Fill four waterpots with water, and pour it on the burnt sacrifice and on the wood." Then he said, "Do it a second time," and they did it a second time; and he said, "Do it a third time," and they did it a third time. So the water ran all around the altar; and he also filled the trench with water.

And it came to pass, at the time of the offering of the evening sacrifice, that Elijah the prophet came near and said, "LORD God of Abraham, Isaac, and Israel, let it be known this day that You are God in Israel and I am Your servant, and that I have done all these things at Your word. Hear me, O LORD, hear me, that this people may know that You are the LORD God, and that You have turned their hearts back to You again."

Then the fire of the LORD fell and consumed the burnt sacrifice, and the wood and the stones and the dust, and it <u>licked up the water that was in the trench</u>. Now when all the people saw it, they fell on their faces; and they said, "The LORD, He is God! The LORD, He is God!"

And Elijah said to them, "Seize the prophets of Baal! Do not let one of them escape!" So they seized them; and Elijah brought them down to the Brook Kishon and executed them there.

1 King 18:30-40 (emphasis added)

My dear friend, do you see what God is saying to us through this event? We have been in a spiritual drought for a very long time, but God is sending His prophets to revive us.

The steps we take are very similar to what Elijah did.

First, he called the people to come close and listen to him. We need to draw near to the teaching of the word and true worship again. Then he made trenches around the sacrifice and filled them with water. We need to be entrenched in our faith and saturated with the water of the word. The word of God will not quench the fire but will be a catalyst to keep the flames of revival burning. We need to cry out to the Holy Spirit with all our hearts to ignite our faith and reveal Himself to us like in the days of old. God will confirm the preaching and teaching of His word with mighty signs and wonders following.

Notice also that Elijah repaired the broken altar using twelve stones which represented the twelve tribes of Israel. What do these stones represent for us? Our new covenant with God and the pillars of our faith in Christ.

In the chapters that follow, I will speak again of our foundations in Christ, starting with the reason Jesus was born, lived and died among us, why the Holy Spirit is with us, the power of the word and all the tools we need to equip us to renew our relationship with the Father and lead transformed lives. If we are to be changed so as to change our own society, we must first return to God's word and His ways.

The story of Elijah does not end here. After that confrontation, he went up the mountain, prayed and listened for the sound of rain. First there was nothing; but on the seventh round there was a cloud the size of a man's hand. Before long, the sky was filled with black clouds and the rain fell in torrents! As you read this book, listen... for the rain!

Let us pray:

> *Dear God,*
> *I am thankful to You today for the opportunity to bring Your word in this way to the world You so love and as the Psalmist said in Psalm 68:11,[4] "The Lord gave the word: great was the company of those that published it." I am grateful to be a part of this great company of publishers. May the readers of this book find a lasting and refreshing inspiration as they engage*

---

[4] KJV

with the content. I bring this prayer in the Name of Jesus Christ, our Lord and soon coming King.
Amen.

Foreword by Bishop Dennis Tanner

I first met the Revd Michael Angley Ogwuche in Glasgow, Scotland in 2009. My wife and I arrived in Glasgow in January of 2009 after I was appointed as the National Overseer for the Church of God in Scotland. Michael was evangelizing in the city, holding special meetings, doing research for a project of AIDS awareness in Scotland, writing a book on AIDS, and was ministering as a chaplain and helping to train other chaplains. He was very active in the ministry and had a tremendous source of energy. Michael was different from other African Christians I had met and worked with, as he was not interested in limiting his ministry to the African community. He had a tremendous burden to reach all citizens of Scotland. He was a minister in our Church of God congregation at the Gorbals, a small area of Glasgow, had started a small fellowship in his home in Lanarkshire, and had opened a charity focusing on social justice in Scotland.

Michael felt that God had brought him to the UK to be a missionary to the people in England and Scotland. He saw the challenge of reaching the Scottish people, who had moved from being a strong Christian influence in the world to a people who now felt very little need for God, the salvation offered by Jesus, or the standards of living taught in the Holy Bible. He was very helpful to me and opened many doors of ministry for the Church of God in Scotland.

This books reflects not only Michael's view but the view of many others of a nation that once prided itself on 'being led by God and with God as the Head of their country' and is now moving beyond post Christian to an anti-Jesus, anti-God and definitely anti-Bible nation. A nation of people that value 'reason and rationality' above 'faith and morality'.

In the book, Michael stresses the importance of getting back to the teaching of the Word of God and true worship. Only then can we see or effect a change in our lives and in our nation. In the first chapter in dealing with belief, Michael emphasizes the importance of not just knowing about someone but actually getting to know them! "I know about the Queen of England, but I do not really know her."

On his chapter on the Holy Spirit, Michael expresses that the Holy Spirit's job or ministry is to help us fully appreciate what Christ came to do and equip and empower us to be witnesses of Jesus Christ to the world. This chapter will encourage the believer that through the Holy Spirit the believer can experience Jesus Christ and His power and really get to 'know' or experience Christ.

As a minister of the gospel, as a classical Pentecostal in my doctrine, and as a Charismatic in my worship, I appreciate what Michael is doing and teaching through the writing of this book, *Preparing for Revival*. Revival will come! Revival can come! Even so, Lord Jesus, start with me! I recommend you read this book and make every effort to apply the principles and teachings in your life. Truly believing, returning to the teaching of the Word of God and true worship, and through the Holy Spirit experiencing who Jesus Christ really is, "...let us renew our covenant with a faithful and just God. Let us rededicate our personal lives, the lives of our children and our nation to Him."

Respectively and humbly submitted,

Bishop Dennis Tanner
Church of God Scotland National Overseer,
Church of God National Office,
Nairn, Scotland, UK, IV12 4NB.

CHAPTER ONE

Do You Really Believe?

As long as you are proud, you cannot know God. A proud man is always looking down on things and people: and, of course, as long as you are looking down you cannot see something that is above you.

C.S. Lewis, Mere Christianity

We are going to start from first principles by looking at the question of belief, and asking ourselves what it is about God we really believe in. First, let us look at the word 'believe'. The Merriam-Webster Dictionary defines belief as "a state or habit of mind in which trust or confidence is placed in some person or thing". Since belief of some kind is central to all faiths, it is impossible to claim to have faith without believing in something.

While most religions have a common set of beliefs, postmodern society tends to personalise truth and say that all truth is relative. There is a subjectivity attached to one's beliefs. In other words, your truth may not be my truth and there is no such thing as *The Truth*. The Bible, on the other hand, is founded on an indisputable set of core truths which come directly from God as revealed to authors inspired by the Holy Spirit. These fundamental beliefs are not open to question. Christians who choose to embrace a personalised view of their faith are in danger of losing touch with the basic teachings of Christianity as outlined in the Bible.

Multiple Views

Ask any casual observer who Jesus is, and you get a variety of opinions. A historical figure who did many good deeds. A wise man. A compassionate person. A prophet who performed miracles. To some, an avatar. Hindus will tell you that there are many paths to reaching God and Jesus Christ is but one of them. Some Jews regard Jesus as but one of the Jewish teachers and no more. For Muslims, Jesus is not the son of God, but he is considered a holy prophet.[5] New Agers will hold on to the view of a universal Christ and Christ-consciousness in the heart of every existing being.

People who profess to be Christians are no less varied in their opinions. Some believe they are Christian because they are right-living, do charitable works and believe in one God. The former Episcopal Bishop of Edinburgh, The Most Rev. Richard Holloway, for example, was quoted by the *Telegraph* as saying, he no longer believed Jesus was the Son of God "literally and biologically" and thought that Jesus was simply "an extraordinary man".[6]

Sometimes we think we really believe, but when it comes to explaining our belief, we are not so sure and cannot defend our faith – much less share it with someone. Sometimes it's very easy to believe when everybody agrees and there is no risk involved. It is more difficult to truly believe when we risk losing something very important: anything from being seen as rational to risking losing our very lives.

At some point in Jesus' ministry it became necessary for Him to ask His followers who they thought He was. He asked them:

> *"Who do people say the Son of Man is?"*
>
> *Matthew 16:13-20 (NIV)*

Even though they had followed Jesus Christ closely for some time and it was expected that they should know the answer to the simple question of the identity of Jesus Christ, they didn't. This is evidenced from the answers they were giving. So, you see that you are not alone if you don't know Jesus that well either yet.

Why do we need to know who Jesus really is? It is very important that followers of Jesus Christ know Him, and well too, because in the Gospel according to John, Jesus Christ says this:

> *"My sheep listen to my voice; I know them, and they follow me. I give them eternal life, and they shall never perish; no one will snatch them out of my hand. My Father, who has given*

---

[5]   Surah Al-Ma'idah 5:75-77, *The Quran* (Birmingham: Maktabah Booksellers and Publisher, 2012), 96

[6]   *https://www.telegraph.co.uk/news/uknews/1315134/Jesus-was-not-the-Son-of-God-says-former-bishop.html*

them to me, is greater than all; no one can snatch them out of my Father's hand."

John 10:27-29 (NIV)

Notice the construction of this passage. There are some important elements to consider: the follower must know who the master is before recognising and listening to the *singular* voice, otherwise they will be listening to *multiple* voices, which clearly are the undoing of many Christians today. As a result of this special relationship between Jesus Christ and His followers, there are special benefits of protection and conditional eternal security, which is the expectation for all believers.

The question then is, how do you know if you really believe? This is not a simple question to answer; you need to come to that place where you can examine yourself and separate what you strongly believe in from what you half-believe in or pay lip service to. Paul encouraged Christians by saying:

Examine yourselves, to see whether you are in the faith. Test yourselves. Or do you not realize this about yourselves, that Jesus Christ is in you?

2 Corinthians 13:5 (ESV)

What should we believe in?

The Bible is very clear concerning what we should believe. Purely and simply, we need to believe that Jesus Christ is the Son of God, sent to be our *only* way to heaven. He is our Redeemer and our Saviour. He is *the* path, not *one of the* paths.

However, in this day of relativism, lest we say we believe in God but find we believe in conflicting things, it might be wise to review the core beliefs concerning Jesus Christ. These separate a true believer from a half-believer or a non-believer.

Let's start by making a few assertions about our faith.

Who Is God?

The first thing we must agree on is our concept of God.

In the beginning God created the heavens and the earth. The earth was without form, and void; and darkness was on the

*face of the deep. And the Spirit of God was hovering over the
face of the waters.*

Genesis 1:1-2 (emphasis added)

The Hebrew word for God is *Elohim*, which is in plural form and
signifies more than one person involved in creation.

Jesus said He is the Son of God, and during His ministry He made
constant reference to the Father and the Holy Spirit. He also taught us to
baptise in the name of the Father, the Son and the Holy Spirit.[7] This is a
collective reference to the triune God. In fact, at the beginning of Jesus'
ministry we have a picture of the Godhead working in unison at the
baptism of Jesus by John the Baptist:

*When He had been baptized, Jesus came up immediately from
the water; and behold, the heavens were opened to Him, and
He saw the Spirit of God descending like a dove and alighting
upon Him. And suddenly a voice came from heaven, saying,
"This is My beloved Son, in whom I am well pleased."*

Matthew 3:16-17

So when we speak of God we have in mind the Triune God, the
Father, the Son who is Jesus Christ and the Holy Spirit. We see in the
first book of the Bible that God is the Creator and we discover many
more of His attributes as we go through the Bible. We will see that the
God of the Bible is the God of the patriarchs – Abraham, Isaac and Jacob
– through that line to King David and through his lineage to Jesus Christ.
The primary way God revealed Himself to man in the Old Testament was
through the Jewish prophets and in the New Testament to all believers
who receive salvation through Jesus Christ.

Who Is Jesus Christ?

The Bible teaches that Jesus Christ is the express image of the invisible
God[8] and that He is God.[9] John in his Gospel writes:

*In the beginning was the Word, and the Word was with God,
and the Word was God. He was with God in the beginning.*

---

[7] See Matthew 28:19
[8] See Colossians 1:15-18
[9] See John 1:1,49

Through Him all things were made; without Him nothing was made that has been made. In Him was life...

John 1:1-4

These are incredibly powerful and theologically profound statements that come only through divine revelation.

John uses the Greek word *logos* for the Word, but rather than the *logos* being an abstract concept, John shows how the Word is so real.

<u>The Word became flesh</u> and made His dwelling among us. We have seen His glory, the glory of the One and Only, who came from the Father, full of grace and truth.

John 1:14 (emphasis added)

That Word is Jesus, God's only begotten Son. When Jesus was born, God entered into our humanity and lived among us. God who is Spirit became visible and touchable in Jesus Christ as He came to share His life with us and show us the nature of God. Again, we see:

For in Christ all the fullness of the Deity lives in bodily form.

Colossians 2:9 (NIV)

Let us examine the next two truths.

First, although Jesus took on a human nature, He was sinless. He was born of a virgin through the power of the Holy Spirit, not through man. We are told that the angel appeared to the virgin Mary to announce that she would conceive through the power of God:

"The Holy Spirit will come upon you, and the power of the Highest will overshadow you; therefore, also, that Holy One who is to be born will be called the Son of God."

Luke 1:35

So Jesus the Son of Man was not conceived in sin like the rest of mankind. We will soon see why He had to be sinless.

The next characteristic of Jesus is that He is fully God and fully man. This divine and human nature is well explained in Philippians 2:6,7 in the Amplified version:

...who, although He existed in the form and unchanging essence of God [as One with Him, possessing the fullness of all the divine attributes—the entire nature of deity] ... emptied Himself [without renouncing or diminishing His deity, but

only temporarily giving up the outward expression of divine equality and His rightful dignity] by assuming the form of a bond-servant, and being made in the likeness of men.

Philippians 2:6,7 (AMP)

You will also remember that when Jesus Christ had risen from the dead, He appeared to the disciples in human form. He ate with them. He showed the scars of His nail-pierced hands and feet as well as the wound on His side to Thomas, who had earlier said he would not believe unless he had seen those marks. Only then did Thomas believe and acknowledge the risen Christ saying, "My Lord and my God!" Jesus said to him:

"Thomas, because you have seen Me, you have believed. Blessed are those who have not seen and yet have believed."

John 20:24-29

Over two thousand years may have passed since that event, but when we believe from the biblical accounts of the resurrection that Jesus is our Lord and our God, we are truly blessed.

I would now like to systematically explain why Jesus had to be sinless and why He had to have a divine as well as a human nature. This takes us back to the Garden of Eden and the Adam and Eve story, but it's worth telling because we need to have a clear understanding of what our redemption is all about.

Adam, which is Hebrew for 'man', was the father of the human race and represents all mankind.[10] He was close to God and was given dominion over all animal and plant life. When Adam sinned, he lost both relationship and dominion.

When he lost his dominion, Satan moved in. All of nature and all the human race came under Satan's control. We see this change of rulership in Luke 4:5-8 when Satan tempted Jesus in the wilderness, offering Him all the kingdoms of this world if only Jesus would bow down and worship him. Jesus refused, but He did not refute the fact that the kingdoms of this world were under Satan's dominion.

That was not the only impact of Adam's fall.

...all have sinned and fall short of the glory of God...

Romans 3:23

---

[10] See Acts 17:26

Adam's sin was legally transferred to all mankind, so all sinned:

> *Therefore, just as through one man sin entered the world, and death through sin, and thus death spread to all men, because <u>all sinned</u> ... Therefore, as through one man's offense judgment came to all men, resulting in condemnation...*
>
> Romans 5:12,18 (emphasis added)

Adam's sin was passed to all mankind and, like it or not, we have all come under Satan's control. Because we have inherited his sin nature, it's in our DNA to sin.

All of us fall short of God's standard of righteousness and holiness.

> *The wages of sin is death.*
>
> Romans 6:23

With the sin of Adam upon us, we were condemned to die spiritually. Our spiritual death would cause us to be eternally separated from God when we die. But, even now, while we are still alive, spiritual decay is taking place. It could be manifested in any number of ways: chronic sickness, emotional instability, breakdown of relationships, a sense of futility. All these are signs of the devil coming to steal, to kill and destroy[11] because we come under his lordship.

Sin has separated us from a holy God.

> *But your iniquities have separated you from your God;*
> *And your sins have hidden His face from you,*
> *So that He will not hear.*
>
> Isaiah 59:2

So, a great chasm exists between God and man. Even so, because we are essentially spirit beings, we yearn to reach Him. Some of us try to reach Him in our own way, for example, through religion, mysticism and yoga, trying to attain a 'higher level of consciousness'. These look like reasonable paths to God because they offer a sense of piety through rituals, prayer, meditation and 'good works' in order to gain merit. They seem right.

But do they appease the righteous anger of God and earn His forgiveness? They don't. Not in God's eyes.

---

[11] See John 10:10

All of us have become like one who is unclean, and all our righteous acts are like filthy rags; we all shrivel up like a leaf, and like the wind our sins sweep us away.

Isaiah 64:6 (NIV)

Furthermore, there is only one way to God and that is through Jesus, God the Son:

"I am the way, the truth, and the life. No one comes to the Father except through Me."

John 14:6

How could Jesus be the only way?

Because sin blocks us from reaching God and sin has to be dealt with. Sin can only be removed when it is atoned for according to God's prescribed method. That method is blood sacrifice:

...almost everything is purified with blood, and <u>without the shedding of blood</u> there is no forgiveness of sins.

Hebrews 9:22 (ESV, emphasis added)

In the Old Testament God allowed animal sacrifice to partially atone for sin each year. But in the fullness of time, He sent His Son to be the perfect sacrifice to bring total forgiveness for all of the sins of all mankind, past, present and future.

For the perfect sacrifice, two vital conditions had to be met:

- the sacrifice of a man to represent all mankind;
- the sacrifice of a sinless man who could stand before a holy God.

The only person on earth who could fulfil these two conditions is Jesus. Jesus became man to represent us. And, as Son of God, He is sinless.

Jesus is the only way.

"I am the way, the truth, and the life. No one comes to the Father except through Me."

John 14:6

We have established that Jesus is the Son of God and He was born without sin. The following scripture testifies to His blameless life:

For He made Him who knew no sin to be sin for us, that we might become the righteousness of God in Him.

2 Corinthians 5:21

He was born a man not only to be the perfect sacrifice. It also gave Him first-hand experience of our human weaknesses. Because He suffered the same temptations and trials we go through, as our High Priest, He understands our weaknesses:

For we do not have a High Priest who cannot sympathize with our weaknesses, but was in all points tempted as we are, yet without sin.

Hebrews 4:15

So Christ had to pay man's penalty for sin by becoming that sin for us at the cross. All the wrath of the Father was thrown at Him through the terrible pain and humiliation He endured:

All we like sheep have gone astray;
We have turned, everyone, to his own way;
And the LORD has laid on Him the iniquity of us all.

Isaiah 53:4,6 (emphasis added)

So terrible was the sin cast upon Him that, for a brief moment, the Father turned His face away from Him, and Jesus cried out:

"Eli, Eli, lama sabachthani?" that is, "My God, My God, why have You forsaken Me?"

Matthew 27:46

But paying the penalty for us with His life was not enough. Jesus had to break the power of sin and death. The wages of sin is death, so He had to overcome death. He did it through His resurrection, thus breaking the stranglehold of death Satan had over us.

Three days after descending into hell, Christ rose again and ascended into heaven. With His own blood, He entered heaven, having obtained eternal life for us through His death and resurrection:

Not with the blood of goats and calves, but with His own blood He entered the Most Holy Place once for all, having obtained eternal redemption.

Hebrews 9:12 (emphasis added)

With His resurrection, His victory over Satan was now complete:

He has delivered us from the power of darkness and conveyed us into the kingdom of the Son of His love, in whom we have redemption through His blood, the forgiveness of sins

Colossians 1:13-14

Jesus' resurrection is well documented. He was seen by His disciples as well as over five hundred witnesses. Many of them touched Him, spoke with Him, ate with Him.

...Christ died for our sins according to the Scriptures, and that He was buried, and that He rose again the third day according to the Scriptures, and that He was seen by Cephas, then by the twelve. After that He was seen by over five hundred brethren at once...

1 Corinthians 15:3-6

Satan, the usurping god of this age, has been defeated. Jesus has reconciled us to God, and we are no longer separated from our Creator. Now we can come to Him as His children, covered with the blood of Jesus. And Jesus is highly exalted for His obedience. He is Lord!

Therefore God also has highly exalted Him and given Him the name which is above every name, that at the name of Jesus every knee should bow, of those in heaven, and of those on earth, and of those under the earth, and that every tongue should confess that Jesus Christ is Lord, to the glory of God the Father.

Philippians 2:9-11

Friends, please understand we cannot come to God based on our good works and merits, as all other religions teach. No, only the blood of a sinless sacrifice – Jesus – can save us. We have to throw ourselves at His feet and ask for His mercy and forgiveness for our sins based on the righteousness of Christ. Salvation is a gift of God and cannot be earned:

For by grace you have been saved through faith, and that not of yourselves; it is the gift of God, not of works, lest anyone should boast.

Ephesians 2:8-9

This, in short, is the gospel of Jesus Christ. If you agree with these core teachings I've shared, that's wonderful. May God bless you! But mental assent is not enough. Even Satan and the demons know the truth about God and tremble.[12]

No, you must receive Jesus in your heart and confess with your mouth that Jesus is your Lord and Saviour. Jesus said that in order to inherit eternal life we must be "born again"[13]. To be born again, we must come to Jesus with a repentant heart and ask Him to change us. If you do this with all sincerity, purposing to follow Jesus and all His ways, a transformation will take place in your spirit. The Holy Spirit will start the work of transforming you into a new creature.[14]

For some, this as a giant step. We will not push it. I will invite you again later. You still have so many questions. One burning question is, how is it that so many people in the world do not believe in Jesus Christ? That is a very valid question that we will cover fully in Chapter 6 when we discuss faith. But for now, the reason is that Satan continues to blind the eyes of the unbeliever to the truth of the gospel lest the light of God should shine upon him.[15] He did that to Eve and he continues to try to deceive all those that allow him.

Let me share a part of my own story.

My Journey of Faith

I was born in the city of Kaduna, northwest Nigeria, in the very late 1960s. My father was a soldier in the Nigeria Army, and we lived in the army barracks. Mother had twelve children with only four of us surviving, of whom I am the youngest. The family setting was competitive and financially tight as a result of multiple wives and mistresses being Father's pastime.

Growing up, it was also an uphill task to find a proper mentor and role model. Not coming from a religious background meant that I had no form of religious experience or affiliation to any faith.

Sometime around 1986 I became obsessed with the idea of getting rich and escaping my poverty-stricken life. However, everything was to change when I started attending a house fellowship of the Deeper Christian Life Ministry, an African Independent Church (AIC) founded by a mathematician turned pastor William F. Kumuyi.

---

[12] See James 2:19
[13] John 3:3
[14] See 2 Corinthians 5:17
[15] See 2 Corinthians 4:4

I happened to be sharing a room at the Army Officers' quarters with a friend called Richard. There was a soldier, Green, who happened to be a Christian, and I came to know him as 'Bro'. Green was trying to share the gospel with Richard, so he visited our room frequently. Unknown to Bro. Green, Richard was not interested in the things of faith but pretended that he was, for some reason best known to him. The manner in which Bro. Green conducted himself caught my attention: not that he was particularly friendly, but I recognised he had some kind of peace within him which I lacked as a result of my struggles.

One day Richard was not at home when Bro. Green came calling. As he turned to leave, I asked him if he only spoke to people who went to his church, and he said no! My response was, "I want to go to church." (The seeker was now evangelizing himself.)

What I found strange was the fact that it was I who initiated the move to invite myself to his church. Many Christians are really not intentional about the mission of God. We often fail to see the spiritual decadence and needs around us each day. If we are intentional about the mission of God and that it is not His will for any to perish, we will always be on the look-out for those poor lost souls (such as I was) and reach out to them to turn them around to God.

I was undoubtedly someone who had perfected the act of sin in my heart, chasing after the things of this world. Young as I was, the quest to escape from my reality was so strong that at that time I was seeking out secret societies that would help me realise my dreams – until I was consumed with these thoughts. But God had His finger on me. God's word aptly states:

> *The heart is more deceitful than all things*
> *and desperately wicked;*
> *who can understand it?*
> *I, the LORD, search the heart,*
> *I test the mind,*
> *even to give to every man according to his ways,*
> *and according to the fruit of his deeds.*
>
> *Jeremiah 17:9-10 (MEV)*

I am convinced that my heart was desperately wicked, yet the love of God found me through one of His unwilling servants, Bro. Green. I was a sinner in need, but God's grace saved me.

Bro. Green invited me to his house fellowship and subsequently his church, and on 12 January 1987 at an evening meeting I responded to an altar call and gave my life to Jesus. It was at this moment that I realised the truth:

> *For God so loved the world that He gave His only begotten Son, that whoever believes in Him should not perish but have everlasting life.*

> *John 3:16*

I also remembered the words of Jesus Christ:

> *...unless one is born again, he cannot see the kingdom of God.*
> *John 3:3b*

I had been to a Catholic Church before, but it could not be compared to having a personal encounter with Jesus Christ. This is an awe-inspiring experience beyond anything I had ever imagined, for, while it is true that Jesus Christ died for the whole world, it is also a personal relationship.

The simple joy in knowing that you are redeemed, secure and restored for the purpose of eternity cannot be compared with anything I had ever experienced. It was exhilarating to know that there is so much more to life. The happy, cheerful and hopeful faces of the believers who came into my life was something I also desired.

I did know about Jesus Christ as a good person who happened to be known as the Son of God. This was something incomprehensible to the unregenerate mind. But I never knew Him for who He is, although I could see His reflection on those who claimed to believe in Him. In my view, this is what Paul was explaining to the Corinthian Church when he talked about the importance of being living witnesses for Christ:

> *The only letter I need is you yourselves! By looking at the good change in your hearts, everyone can see that we have done a good work among you. They can see that you are a letter from Christ, written by us. It is not a letter written with pen and ink, but by the Spirit of the living God; not one carved on stone, but in human hearts.*

> *2 Corinthians 3:2-3 (TLB)*

It's possible to know about a person without knowing that person. For example, like many, I know a lot about the Queen of England, yet I have never met her and therefore, I cannot claim that I know her; neither does she know me. In the same way, knowing about Jesus Christ is not the same as knowing Him. Each day since the day I said yes to the primary call to be His follower, I have never stopped getting to know more of Him through prayer, studying the Bible and fellowshipping with other believers.

I cannot agree more with Paul when he says:

> *For we know in part and we prophesy in part, but when completeness comes, what is in part disappears. When I was a child, I talked like a child, I thought like a child, I reasoned like a child. When I became a man, I put the ways of childhood behind me. For now we see only a reflection as in a mirror; then we shall see face to face. Now I know in part; then I shall know fully, even as I am fully known.*
>
> *1 Corinthians 13:9-12 (NIV)*

I believe we do not need to know Jesus before accepting His call. The journey of knowing Jesus begins the moment we say, "Yes!" Some people think that the prerequisite for being a Christian is to have some kind of affinity with Him, either through our upbringing or associations, before they can come. But, *no,* the journey begins the moment you say yes. Even right now.

Do you want to live a powerful victorious life? Do you want to overcome your seemingly defeat? Do you want to rise above your obsessions? In the next chapter I am going to show you how. We will look more closely at the benefits of the cross and the power of the blood of Jesus.

CHAPTER TWO

The Power of the Cross

Rejoice greatly, O daughter Zion!
Shout aloud, O daughter Jerusalem!

Zechariah 9:9

Come along as I narrate three episodes relating to the most life-transforming events in history: the crucifixion and resurrection of our Saviour Jesus Christ, which are the central character of our Christian faith. This discourse is by no means a systematic theological narrative; instead, it contains insights from personal understanding gained through relationship with God, and the application of the word of God through the inspiration of the Holy Spirit. May the words and imagery contained in the narrative stimulate your spirit as we seek together to follow in the steps of Jesus Christ on the road to Calvary.

The Triumphant Entry

Can I encourage you to start by reading Luke 19:29-40? It gives us insight into some of the circumstances leading to Christ's crucifixion.

Death by crucifixion was the Roman authorities' way of punishing criminals as well as instilling fear in the hearts of potential offenders. Jesus Christ had to experience it as He was accused of attempting to derail an already fragile polity. It wasn't long before His activities came under the radar of the socio-political and religious establishments. In addition to the Romans' accusation, the Jews also had plausible reasons for wanting to confront Jesus and destroy His ministry.

It seems that Jesus' disposition set Him up to look as if He were on a collision course with the authority of the regional Roman Governor. Although at this time there was heightened messianic expectation by the Jewish community, Jesus did not seem to meet the criteria of the predicted and expected Messiah. He challenged both secular and sacred authorities. He also went against the grain by choosing supposedly two natural enemies: Simon the Zealot, whose ideologies were against the occupying Roman oppressive government; and Matthew, a civil servant in the same government. These and other similar actions pitched Jesus Christ against the two opposing entities. On the side of the expectant Jews there was also no clear consensus about how exactly the Messiah would be. However, it is easy to decipher that a considerable segment of the Jewish population was expecting a king in the fashion of David as foretold by some prophets.

The other Gospels telling of Jesus' entry into Jerusalem[16] have the familiar features of 'palm fronds and Hosannas' but in Luke's account there are no palms and no hosannas; instead we are told that cloaks are laid out for Jesus Christ to ride His donkey on. Luke noted that the surrounding voices were from Jesus' own disciples; this also slightly contrasts with the other Gospel reports in that Luke did not report the dissenting voices who in a few days would call for Jesus' crucifixion.

SIGNIFICANCE OF THE TRIUMPHANT ENTRY

Although not noted in Luke, we are told by commentators that it is quite likely that there was another boisterous entry on the day that Jesus Christ entered into Jerusalem, even though it was political. Entering first was the Roman Governor from the West with full military tattoo of might, amour, swords, chariots and with all other possible paraphernalia, including an elaborate chariot carrying Pilate himself. Can you imagine the stark contrast on Jesus' side as He enters Jerusalem on the back of a colt (a small donkey) – and yet *unlike Pilate, Jesus Christ brings not fear and oppression but much hope, joy and peace?* On one hand, Pilate represents the kingdom of man; on the other, Christ represents the kingdom of God.

These two events had both political and religious dimensions to them; one was popular, reasonable and appropriate with spectacular pageantry, while the other had no pomp but was full of humility and peace. As usual, the population had to choose where to pitch their tents between these two opposing parties. The sensitive nature of Jesus' entry into Jerusalem was obvious and such a situation could have easily escalated into premature altercation in the city. The scheduling of such an event to coincide with Pilate's entourage from the other side could not have been

---

[16]   Matthew 21:1-11; Mark 11:9; Luke 19:28-44

more distasteful to the Roman authority and counterproductive for Jesus' welcome party, especially as it was the convention of kings to ride a donkey into a city; the oppressive Roman Government, who had no place for new kings or another power, would have considered Jesus' triumphant entry a serious potential threat to their dominance in the region. Again, as noted earlier, the implication of this seeming coincidence is that Jesus knew the timing and how appropriate it was; therefore, it was not exactly a *coincidence* but rather a *'divine incidence'* for the Lord of lords and the King of kings to ride majestically on a peace symbol into the city of God.

The story shows clearly that "all power belongs to God, now and forever"[17] and all authorities are from Him. The Bible says:

> *[God] determines the number of the stars;*
> *he gives to all of them their names.*
> *Great is our Lord, and abundant in power;*
> *his understanding is beyond measure.*
>
> *Psalm 147:4-5 (ESV)*

The crowd threw their cloaks and palm branches into the street. I can imagine it in my head and relate to this scene. Jesus' disciples understood the significance of the visit and they were thrown into ecstasy. They shouted, "Blessed is the king who comes in the name of the Lord,"[18] and, "Peace in heaven and glory in the highest!" [19] This must have been great news for those expectant Jews: *the Messiah is finally here!* But some in the crowd must also have been worried because they didn't want to incur the anger of the Roman government; only the Emperor enjoyed such accolade. There were also others within the religious hierarchy that did not consider Jesus Christ as the long-expected Messiah; He did not fit the pattern, so they added to the chorus, "Teacher, rebuke Your disciples!"

As non-participant observers of these events and separated in culture and time, we can still learn some useful lessons from the story. Our society today is filled with a variety of opinions – popular and unpopular, whether political, religious, spiritual or social. We are constrained to choose between what is godly and what is socially acceptable by the society we live in.

---

[17] 1 Peter 5:11
[18] Luke 19:38a
[19] Luke 19:38b

But the point to note here is that the popular, reasonable and appropriate opinions may not necessarily be the right ones; instead the unpopular and sometime politically and socially incorrect ones may be what God requires of us.

The question we must ask of ourselves is, are we going to:

- choose to be in Jesus' welcome party and chorus, "Blessed is the king who comes in the name of the Lord! ... Peace in heaven and glory in the highest!";
- join the Pharisaic crowd in the same welcome party and ask Jesus Christ, "Teacher, rebuke your disciples!";
- move over entirely to Pilate's side?

It would have been safer to join the popular welcome party of the Roman authority rather than join that of Jesus Christ because anything else would have been interpreted as supporting a possible rebellion against the Roman rulers. But they had to make up their minds as to whom they would follow – and some actually did; they welcomed the lone young donkey rider, waving and shouting and paving the ground He rode on with their cloaks. After all, it was prophesied:

> *Rejoice greatly, Daughter Zion! Shout, Daughter Jerusalem!*
> *See, your king comes to you, righteous and victorious, lowly*
> *and riding on a donkey, on a colt, the foal of a donkey.*
>
> *Zechariah 9:9*

We too have a choice to make as we acknowledge the passion of Jesus Christ in our lives and accept that Calvary was for us and that Jesus' resurrection at Easter gives us hope in this world and in the world to come. By so doing, we will make not the popular and politically correct choices but the right one which is according to the plan of God for our salvation.

"Hosanna in the Highest!"

From Mark's account the ecstatic crowds lay their clothes and palm branches before Him, proclaiming Jesus as King with shouts of "Hosanna! Blessed is He who comes in the name of the LORD!" How swiftly things change from shouts of "Hosanna!" to cries of "Crucify Him!" by the end of the week.

The word *hosanna* is a transliteration of two Hebrew words, *hoshiya* and *na,* that together mean, "Save us, we pray," or, "Save, please!" It is based on Psalm 118 and was proclaimed as an expression of confidence in the Lord, praising and thanking God for the help received in times of distress.

Looking at both Mark and Luke, we are led to ask whether the circumstances leading to the trial, crucifixion and subsequent resurrection of Jesus Christ were a sign of weakness or strength. His followers were scattered, fearful and full of despair. They had walked with Jesus for three years believing in Him and trusting in His words. Now He was cruelly snatched away from them. But, look again: sandwiched between Good Friday and Resurrection Sunday there is an inconspicuous *Holy Saturday,* a sliver of hope, a pause in the midst of uncertainty and vulnerability. Could those who knew their God and His mighty acts in the past dare to revisit the promises in the scriptures concerning the king?

> *And the government will be upon His shoulder.*
> *And His name will be called*
> *Wonderful, Counselor, Mighty God,*
> *Everlasting Father, Prince of Peace.*
>
> *Isaiah 9:6*

Did God have a bigger and better plan for the Jews? Yes, beyond their imagination. This was not a temporary rescue from a political oppressor but an eternal plan for all mankind to be delivered from the powers of darkness and to live that abundant life He had come to give them. That prophetic word spoken by the prophet Isaiah some seven hundred years earlier continues:

> *Of the increase of His government and peace*
> *There will be no end,*
> *Upon the throne of David and over His kingdom,*
> *To order it and establish it with judgment and justice*
> *From that time forward, even forever*
> *The zeal of the LORD of hosts will perform this.*
>
> *Isaiah 9:7*

Yes, the government of your affairs and mine is on His shoulders. He is in control of all things, even those that overwhelm us. If He could carry the weight of the world on His shoulders, He will carry us too. He is our

Wonderful Counsellor, Mighty God, Everlasting Father, Prince of Peace. His kingdom is in you and, when you open your heart to Him, He will give you His peace. He will ultimately establish judgment and justice in our lives and in our nation for ever.

In that quiet pause moment between defeat and victory, as we hold on to that prophecy, may we all who believe bond together as we look expectantly to Him and His promises.

> *Rejoice greatly, O daughter Zion! Shout aloud, O daughter Jerusalem! Lo, your king comes to you; triumphant and victorious is he, humble and riding on a donkey, on a colt, the foal of a donkey.*

> *Zechariah 9:9*

Little did the people know, but their hosanna was a prophetic act. It meant one thing for them, but all heaven was shouting in agreement because heaven knew the reality of that ride on a donkey to that city of David that day. The reality was that Jesus Christ was indeed entering Jerusalem as Son of David, King and Messiah. He was the rightful King coming to claim His kingdom.

Hosanna in the highest, for Your redemption has come!

"It Is Finished!"

Some Christians like to shy away from the actual events that took place on Good Friday because of their graphic nature. But, however politically correct we would like to be, no one can take the gruesomeness of Calvary away, because the fact still remains. We need not be apologetic about the brutality of what actually transpired at the cross and the events leading up to it.

David the Psalmist, speaking prophetically four hundred years before, already picked up that anguished cry which could only have come from Jesus:

> *My God, my God, why have you forsaken me?*
> *Why are you so far from saving me,*
>   *so far from my cries of anguish?*
> *My God, I cry out by day,*
>   *but you do not answer,*
>   *by night, but I find no rest.*

> *Psalm 22:1*

The four Gospel writers were not afraid to report its graphic detail, so why should we be? We need not only to *hear* about what happened to Jesus but also to *think seriously* about it and let it sink deep down into our hearts, if we want to experience the full benefits of the cross and the resurrection.

THE GORY DETAILS

Take a moment to read Matthew 27, Mark 15, Luke 23 and John 19.

The Romans are widely believed to be the inventors of execution by crucifixion; they were so proficient in it that it became part of their proud history. Because Christ was condemned to die under the Roman system, it was only natural that He should die by crucifixion outside the city walls.

The Roman soldiers whipped Jesus to the count of thirty-nine lashes across His back. If you've seen the movie *The Passion of the Christ* you will understand the pain of having whips attached with sharp pieces object that tear at His flesh. They placed a crown of thorns piercing His head. Then He was made to carry His cross to Golgotha.

In our world today even the most hardened of criminals deserve some human dignity or rights, but these were not accorded to the King of kings. The taunting crowd made matters worse for this badly beaten man as He made His way slowly through the streets. By now He was totally exhausted, until Simon of Cyrene was forced to assist.

Jesus was thirsty and they gave Him a sponge dipped in vinegar mixed with myrrh, which He refused. Then He was nailed to the cross between two felons. It was brutal, bloody and torturous, aggravated by the jeering crowd, the slapping and spitting, the chief priests and elders defying Him to save Himself, the soldiers joking and rolling dice for His seamless robe as He was stripped naked to hang on the cross in sight of all.

Psalm 22 captures exactly the thoughts that were running through His mind. As you read the rest of this passage, can you see the alternating emotions of abandonment, adoration and humiliation as He cries out to the Father?

> *Yet you are enthroned as the Holy One;*
> *you are the one Israel praises.*
> *In you our ancestors put their trust;*
> *they trusted, and you delivered them.*

To you they cried out and were saved;
in you they trusted and were not put to shame.
But I am a worm and not a man,
scorned by everyone, despised by the people.
All who see me mock me;
they hurl insults, shaking their heads.
'He trusts in the LORD,' they say,
'let the LORD rescue him.
Let him deliver him, since he delights in him.'

Psalm 22:1-8 (NIVUK)

We have to remind ourselves that although the death of Jesus Christ was a malicious miscarriage of justice, it was absolutely a divine necessity. It was God's will for Jesus Christ to die for the remission of our sins. Hebrews 9:22 succinctly states:

…under the law, it's almost the case that everything is purified
in connection with blood; without the shedding of blood, sin
cannot be forgiven.

Hebrews 9:22 (TVT)

That is good news! But why the pain?

Yes, why the torture, you may ask. Couldn't the execution be performed swiftly so as to minimise the pain? Wouldn't that be sufficient to appease the righteous requirements of the law? Is such brutality a reflection of the God of love?

There is much to ponder about in the key verse of Isaiah 53.

Surely he took up our pain and bore our suffering, yet we
considered him punished by God, stricken by him, and
afflicted. But he was <u>*pierced*</u> *for our transgressions, he was*
<u>*crushed*</u> *for our iniquities; the* <u>*punishment*</u> *that brought us*
peace was on him, and by his <u>*wounds*</u> *we are healed.*

Isaiah 53:4-5 (KJV, emphasis added)

He was "pierced", "crushed" and "by his wounds we are healed". That says a host of things to us. Jesus was whipped by thirty-nine strokes of the lash. By His wounds we are healed of all physiological conditions. Add to that the physical torture, the mocking, the humiliation of being stripped naked, the outrage of being falsely accused, the rejection of His

41

followers, and we have all our emotional pain that He took upon Himself as punishment as well.

But by far the worst pain He suffered was the sense of seeming abandonment by the Father at the time of His greatest need. He who knew no sin became sin for us. The Father's face was turned away from Him, such was the magnitude of the sins of all humanity. That moment of alienation must have been the hardest blow, as He cried out:

> *My God, my God, why hast thou forsaken me?*
>
> *Matthew 27:46 (KJV)*

The pain of separation was mutual, experience by the Father as well as the Son. But it had to be experienced for our sakes so that we would never have to go through the route of all human dysfunctions: rejection.

> *But it was the LORD's good plan to crush him*
> *   and cause him grief.*
> *Yet when his life is made an offering for sin,*
> *   he will have many descendants.*
> *He will enjoy a long life,*
> *   and the LORD's good plan will prosper in his hands.*
> *When he sees all that is accomplished by his anguish,*
> *   he will be satisfied.*
>
> *Isaiah 53:10-11 (NLT)*

His suffering went beyond payment for sin. He stood for every sickness and every painful emotion that we might experience in life: rejection, shame, guilt, unworthiness, abuse, fear, bewilderment, poverty, hopelessness. Now we do not have to carry those burdens on our own. The Bible says that when we make His life an offering to God on our behalf, we will enjoy long life and will prosper. If we contemplate on the profundity of that truth, we will find that that sacrificial giving of Himself was, in itself, demonstration of love at its maximum. The Scripture says that God loved the world so much that He gave... *everything!*[20] For us to have everything! What manner of love is this if not *agape*[21]?

It is finished!

---

[20] See John 3:16

[21] *Agape* (Ancient Greek): word for divine love, exercised between God and man

Where possible, the last words of any dying person may be the most important words for the family as that will be where the secret treasures are revealed; such words are always remembered and cherished by those who heard them. For Jesus Christ, His was, "It is finished!"[22] and we the family cherish those last words; they contain the greatest revelation which has the potency to revise the trajectory of the world for good, especially the world of those who will believe in them. These words simply mean, "Here is the conclusion of all matters pertaining to your sin and suffering, because I did this for you. I did this once and for all!"

> *He entered once for all time into the most holy place—entering, not with the blood of goats or calves or some other prescribed animal but offering His own blood and thus obtaining redemption for us for all time.*
>
> *Hebrews 9:12 (TVT)*

Those last words of Jesus did not just come from a helpless dying and defeated man, but from a conqueror who gave His all for us. Our response to the trial, suffering and the death of Jesus Christ, therefore, should be from the same position of victory and, more importantly, in the sure knowledge that victory will be completed in the resurrection. What is good about Good Friday is that *it is finished!*

OUR RESPONSE

Our burdens were lifted at Calvary because on that cross was:

- *our sin* – Jesus carried our sin (2 Corinthians 5:21);
- *our lack of peace* – the chastisement of our peace was upon Jesus (Isaiah 53:5);
- *our curses* – our iniquities were laid upon Jesus at the cross (Isaiah 53:6);
- *our sicknesses* – by His stripes they were healed (1 Peter 2:24).

You are invited to embrace the full benefits of the finished work of Calvary and run with them. To do so you must make conscious effort:

- *never to worry about your past*

---

[22] John 19:30

Nothing in our past can condemn us once we are in Christ.[23]
The cross reaches into our past! There are those in God's service
who feel they have no right to be blessed or used in His service
because of the guilt of past wrongs. But I say, precisely because
of the price Jesus paid, you do have a right to worship and serve
Him. The cross of Jesus gives you that right; therefore,
paradoxically, our past should not determine our future, because
it is the absolute wish of God for us to prosper.

*But as many as received Him, to them He gave the right to
become children of God, to those who believe in His name:
who were born, not of blood, nor of the will of the flesh, nor
of the will of man, but of God.*

John 1:12-13

- *never to worry about your present*
  There is nothing in the present that can hinder or rob us once we
  have come to the cross of Christ. Whatever we are facing, Jesus
  is the answer. Of course, we will be called upon to bear the
  crosses of life's circumstances, but Jesus bore the cross that
  matters most. The Apostle Paul writes:

*For I have every confidence that nothing—not death, life,
heavenly messengers, dark spirits, the present, the future,
spiritual powers, height, depth, nor any created thing—can
come between us and the love of God revealed in the
Anointed, Jesus our Lord.*

Romans 8:38-39 (TVT)

- *never to worry about your future*
  Our future is secure in Christ as we look steadily to "Jesus the
  pioneer and perfecter of faith"[24]. God didn't just call you to
  conversion. He didn't just call you to regeneration. He didn't
  just call you to be justified. He called you to His eternal glory.
  That's why Jesus spoke of the many mansions in His Father's
  house He was preparing for us.[25]

---

[23] See Romans 8:1
[24] Hebrews 12:2 (NIV)
[25] See John 14:2

The greatest note of victory ever broadcast in the ears of a stunned creation was the one sounded on the cross of Christ: "It is finished!" That is the final word in the redemption of humankind.

Jesus Christ became a curse and the divinely acceptable sacrifice for us, and thus Calvary is the measure of God's wrath and God's love expressed concurrently. But the greater of these is love.

The finished work of Calvary seals our fate and establishes our faith in Jesus Christ forever; we are never to remain the same again. Our transformation is not designed to deform but to inform and reform us. Real spiritual transformation happens in our state of vulnerability with God at work because God sees the bigger picture.

His Is Risen!

THE FIRST WITNESSES

The resurrection happened quietly and unobtrusively in the early hours of Sunday morning. Only heaven stood witness to this, together with the two angels who had sat on either side of the body of Christ guarding Him, a living enactment of the two cherubim on either side of the mercy seat in the tabernacle of old.[26]

The first signs that Jesus was risen were picked up by a selected few, and what they represent is significant. In the Gospel of Luke we read that the women who were present at the crucifixion visited the tomb early the next morning bringing spices to anoint the body. Seeing the stone rolled away, they entered the tomb and saw that Jesus' body was missing. In alarm they looked up and saw two men in shining garments who say to them, "Why do you seek the living among the dead? He is not here, but is risen!"[27]

The women rush back to break the news to the disciples but their words are dismissed as 'idle tales' by most. Peter gets up though, and runs to the tomb, where he sees the linen cloths lying by themselves; he leaves in wonder at what has happened.[28]

In ancient Jewish society women were considered second-class citizens. But they are named in Luke 24:10 and we recognise one of them as Mary Magdalene, the one who anointed Jesus with expensive perfume

---

[26] See John 20:12
[27] Luke 24:1-12
[28] See Luke 24:11,12

before burial. They were the ones who had stood faithfully at the cross weeping for Him when everyone else had deserted Him. In a fuller account in the Gospel of John, it is Mary Magdalene who is highlighted, and she meets the risen Christ outside the tomb. This account also mentions the beloved disciple John himself, who runs to the tomb with Peter, the same John who remained at the cross supporting the mother of Jesus.[29]

To the outsider these people are nonentities, or at least ordinary people who had not distinguished themselves by anything noteworthy. But God chooses the foolish things of this world to shame the wise, the weak things of the world to put to shame the things which are mighty.[30] As for Peter, here was a man who had fallen from grace and had lost his credibility because of his denial of Jesus.

> *A broken and a contrite heart, these He will not despise.*
>
> *Psalm 51:17*

God saw the servant hearts of their people and their longing to reunite with Him, and counted them worthy to be the ones He would first reveal Himself to. Not to the Sanhedrin or teachers of the law, but to the weak and foolish. For to the sane and worldly wise, the resurrection would be in the same category as the virgin birth, the miracles of Jesus and the parting of the Red Sea – phenomena that needed to meet the scrutiny of science or else be rejected.

My friend, do not be ashamed of your love for Jesus and longing for intimacy with Him, for He will share His secrets with you, too.

That same day Jesus appeared to the eleven disciples who were able to verify that it was indeed the same Jesus who had walked with them, albeit in a glorified body that could pass through walls. They touched Jesus, put their hands in His wounds and heard His voice, fed His hunger and received His blessing. Then they, even doubting Thomas, believed. And then Jesus appeared to many of His followers over forty days till the time He ascended into heaven.

THE ROAD TO EMMAUS

Early that same morning, two of Jesus' disciples were returning to their village, Emmaus. Their hopes had been crushed. The man they

---

29   See John 20:1-18; John 19:26
30   See 1 Corinthians 1:27

believed in had been executed like a common criminal and was now dead. Even after three days, according to the promise, nothing had happened, though rumours were circulating that He was alive.

They are joined by a stranger whom they do not recognise. As Jesus listens to their story, He admonishes them for their lack of faith:

> *"O foolish ones, and slow of heart to believe in all that the prophets have spoken! Ought not the Christ to have suffered these things and to enter into His glory?" And beginning at Moses and all the Prophets, He expounded to them in all the Scriptures the things concerning Himself.*
>
> Luke 24:25-27

On reaching the village, they invite Him to stay the night, and here's where the revelation comes.

> *Now it came to pass, as He sat at the table with them, that He took bread, blessed and broke it, and gave it to them. Then their eyes were opened and they knew Him; and He vanished from their sight.*
>
> *And they said to one another, "Did not our heart burn within us while He talked with us on the road, and while He opened the Scriptures to us?"*
>
> Luke 24:30-32

A new strength comes. They gather themselves together and return to Jerusalem to proclaim that the Lord had risen indeed, and how He was made known to them in the breaking of bread.[31]

This story should encourage all those who are weary and feel like giving up. Go back to the word you heard and to God's promises in whatever situation you face till the word burns in your heart. Don't listen to what your mind tells you; listen to your heart. He will surely lift you up and put you on track again. You may have been heading in the wrong direction to your place of comfort, but God is strengthening you again for the work that He has for you – in the centre of His will.

---

[31] See Luke 20:30-35

Why Is the Resurrection Significant?

The resurrection is the foundation of the Christian faith because it centres on the belief that Jesus Christ not only died on the cross but that He rose from the dead. That reality authenticates the entire message of Christ. It confirms that Jesus is the God of creation and giver of life, that He came into this world to destroy the works of the devil and that He has shown us the way to a victorious and abundant life.

A once timid Peter stood in the power of the Holy Spirit and preached one of the most compelling evangelistic sermons ever to a gathering of thousands of people, resulting in three thousand people being saved. What was the crux of the sermon? The victorious resurrection of Jesus Christ from the dead.

> *"God has raised this Jesus to life, and we are all witnesses of it. Exalted to the right hand of God, he has received from the Father the promised Holy Spirit and has poured out what you now see and hear."*
>
> *Acts 2:32-34 (NIV)*

The resurrection was therefore the single event in the days of the early church that gave impetus to the spread of the gospel. It was clear evidence that the crucifixion of Jesus was not a tragedy but a triumph. The early followers of Christ saw themselves as "witnesses to the resurrection"[32]. Peter and John created pandemonium among the religious elite because they were preaching about Jesus and the resurrection[33] and the apostles testified to this with great power.[34]

Wherever he went Paul preached the "good news about Jesus and the resurrection"[35]. His teaching was based on not only the resurrection of Jesus Christ but the *resurrection of all men.*

> *Now if Christ is preached that He has been raised from the dead, how do some among you say that there is no resurrection of the dead? But if there is no resurrection of the dead, then Christ is not risen. And if Christ is not risen, then our preaching is empty and your faith is also empty. Yes, and*

---

[32] Acts 1:15-16
[33] See Acts 4:1-2
[34] See Acts 4:33
[35] Acts 17:18

we are found false witnesses of God, because we have testified of God that He raised up Christ, whom He did not raise up— if in fact the dead do not rise. For if the dead do not rise, then Christ is not risen. And if Christ is not risen, your faith is futile; you are still in your sins! Then also those who have fallen asleep in Christ have perished. If in this life only we have hope in Christ, we are of all men the most pitiable.

1 Corinthians 15:12-19

The resurrection of Jesus from the dead is the forerunner of the resurrection of our own mortal bodies. Just as Jesus has conquered death and the power of sin, so also has He conquered death for all who are in Christ. Therefore, sin has no longer any hold over those in Christ.

For sin is the sting that results in death, and the law gives sin its power. But thank God! He gives us victory over sin and death through our Lord Jesus Christ.

1 Corinthians 15:56-57

The resurrection is also the single phenomenon that distinguishes Christianity from other faiths. According to the World Christian Encyclopedia, there are nearly 10,000 distinct religions in the world today. However, while all religions seek to satisfy man's desire to reach God, it is only the Christian faith that has an authentic death, burial and resurrection narrative attested by many verifiable and credible sources, proving Jesus' claim. The experience common to man is death, and death has become man's focal point. If all life ends in death or reincarnation of some form, what is the transformative power attached to that faith when there is no accountability for our works on earth? Only the resurrection of our bodies makes us intentional about how we live this life, for the Bible says:

"...it is appointed for men to die once, but after this the judgment."

Hebrews 9:27

We continue to be reminded by this intriguing story that Jesus lives to announce to the world that we (His body) are an exclusive creation of God with an important role to play in the mission of God on earth. In the eyes of God, we are the pearl of great price,[36] considered to be the fruit of the resurrection.

CONCLUSION

The resurrection is an invitation to you who believe to receive what Christ has prepared for you. Christ's offer of eternal life is a gift that must be received. To you who are yet to acknowledge and accept the invitation, please be reminded that *today* is the day of salvation, right here, right now. But the choice is absolutely yours because God created you as a free-will moral agent.

The Bible says:

> *...if you confess with your mouth the Lord Jesus and believe in your heart that God has raised Him from the dead, you will be saved. For with the heart one believes unto righteousness, and with the mouth confession is made unto salvation.*
>
> Romans 10:9,10

If that is your desire, then make a conscious effort today and ask Jesus Christ to come into your heart where you are. Jesus said:

> *"Now pay attention; I am standing at the door and knocking. If any of you hear My voice and open the door, then I will come in to visit with you and to share a meal at your table, and you will be with Me."*
>
> Revelation 3:20 (TVT)

God is waiting for your prayer of acceptance because He loves you enough to have paid the price of your redemption through Jesus Christ. If you have made that decision in prayer today, then find a company of believers who can help you grow and become a part of it, and the Holy Spirit will guide you through the rest of your journey.

---

[36] See Matthew 13:45-46

CHAPTER THREE

The Power of the Holy Spirit

"And I will pray the Father, and He will give you another Helper, that He may abide with you forever—the Spirit of truth."

John 14:16

In the first chapter we discussed the Triune God, as Father in creation, Son in redemption and Holy Spirit in regeneration, albeit with capability of manifesting as needed.

God's plan is very great as we all know. Here it is: we saw God as a man; God's Spirit proved he was right; angels saw him; the nations were told about him; people of the world believed in him; God took him up into heaven.

1 Timothy 3:16 (WE)

From the beginning of time God's Spirit has been involved in all aspects of creation.

...the earth was waste and void; and darkness was upon the face of the deep: and the Spirit of God moved upon the face of the waters.

Genesis 1:2

There has been no stage in human history in which the Spirit of God was not active.

The Holy Spirit played a major role in the lives of many Old Testament leaders and prophets, revealing God's plans, inspiring the writing of the Bible and coming upon them to do mighty acts – from Moses, to David, to Joel and Malachi. But there is a watershed between the Holy Spirit experience of the Old Testament and in the new covenant where all believers are privileged to receive that power if they ask for it.

Bible prophecy says there will be an outpouring of the Holy Spirit "on all flesh" in these last days and we must prepare ourselves for this final dramatic move of God:

> And it shall come to pass afterward
> That I will pour out My Spirit on all flesh;
> Your sons and your daughters shall prophesy,
> Your old men shall dream dreams,
> Your young men shall see visions.
> And also on My menservants and on My maidservants
> I will pour out My Spirit in those days.
>
> *Joel 2:28-29*

It is therefore vital that we have a clear understanding of the role of the Holy Spirit among believers since Pentecost. We must come with expectancy and boldness. Tradition may say one thing, but God's word never fails. So do not allow anyone to hold you back from what God has in store for you.

Preparation

On the eve of His departure from earth, Jesus Christ began to tell His disciples about the Holy Spirit who takes the role of comforter, because in His foreknowledge, He knew that His followers would need that power before they could be effective in their calling. It was going to be a time of great distress and uncertainty for them. He gave them these words of comfort:

> "...I will send the Holy Spirit upon you, just as my Father promised. Don't begin telling others yet—stay here in the city until the Holy Spirit comes and fills you with power from heaven."
>
> *Luke 24:49 (TLB)*

And in the Book of Acts He tells them:

> "But when the Holy Spirit has come upon you, you will receive power to testify about me with great effect, to the people in Jerusalem, throughout Judea, in Samaria, and to the ends of the earth, about my death and resurrection."
>
> *Acts 1:8 (TLB)*

At this stage Jesus reveals only as much their emotions can assimilate. In fact, the Greek text renders the Holy Spirit beautifully as *parakletos*, literally, 'the One who walks alongside of us'. He is our Helper, Comforter, Counsellor, the Spirit of truth, who would teach us all things and bring to remembrance the words of Jesus:

> *"And I will pray the Father, and He will give you another Helper, that He may abide with you forever—the Spirit of truth, whom the world cannot receive, because it neither sees Him nor knows Him; but you know Him, for He dwells with you and will be in you. I will not leave you orphans; I will come to you ... He will teach you all things, and bring to your remembrance all things that I said to you."*
>
> *John 14:16-18,26*

These words were especially comforting to His followers when they realised that they would never be abandoned. As Jesus had a close relationship with His followers, so will we when we welcome the Holy Spirit into our lives. As part of the last days outpouring, the Holy Spirit also will convict sinners of sin, of judgment and unrighteousness.[37] Above all, the Holy Spirit will reveal and glorify Jesus Christ to us in a deeper way.[38]

But there is something in Jesus' words they might have missed:

> *"...but you know Him, for He dwells <u>with</u> you and will be <u>in</u> you."*
>
> *John 14:17 (emphasis added)*

The word 'with' rather than 'in' signifies the difference between the Holy Spirit dwelling *among* the old covenant saints and *in* new covenant believers; this is called the 'in-filling'.

Scholars debate whether the in-filling of the Holy Spirit happens at the time of receiving Jesus or on receiving the baptism of the Holy Spirit. It might be true of both, the difference being a matter of degree. It was this in-filling of the Holy Spirit the disciples received when the resurrected Jesus appeared to them.

---

[37] See John 16:8-11
[38] See John 16:14

> *He breathed on them, and said to them, "Receive the Holy Spirit. If you forgive the sins of any, they are forgiven them; if you retain the sins of any, they are retained."*
>
> *John 20:22-23*

Some see this act as symbolic, anticipating Pentecost. Others see it as an immediate commissioning of the disciples both to preach salvation (as confirmed in Matthew 28:18-20 and Mark 16:15-18) as well as to release or withhold forgiveness of sin depending on the hearer's response. And just as the breath of God marked the first breath of life given to man in Genesis 1, this second breath would mark the beginning of the terms of the new covenant.

Perfect Agreement

It is important to establish that as the Spirit of truth, whatever the Holy Spirit reveals to us will confirm the word, which is Jesus. The Holy Spirit is in agreement with the Father and in agreement with Jesus.[39] Therefore He will bear witness of who Jesus says He is and what Jesus says in His word. In no way will He deviate from it. Jesus continues:

> *"But when the Helper comes, whom I shall send to you from the Father, the Spirit of truth who proceeds from the Father, He will testify of Me."*
>
> *John 15:26*

> *"However, when He, the Spirit of truth, has come, He will guide you into all truth; for He will not speak on His own authority, but whatever He hears He will speak; and He will tell you things to come. He will glorify Me, for He will take of what is Mine and declare it to you."*
>
> *John 16:13-14*

This is crucial because if you are not sure whether you heard from the Holy Spirit, always come back to the word to see whether it is in agreement with it. John the Apostle, writing to the early church, warns us to test every spirit to see whether they are of God or the evil one.

> *Beloved, do not believe every spirit, but test the spirits to see whether they are from God, for many false prophets have gone*

---

[39] See John 17

out into the world. By this you know the Spirit of God: every spirit that confesses that Jesus Christ has come in the flesh is from God, and every spirit that does not confess Jesus is not from God. This is the spirit of the antichrist, which you heard was coming and now is in the world already.

1 John 4:1-3 (ESV)

Since Jesus is the word of God and every word spoken by Jesus is true, if you hear a spirit say anything which is contrary to the word, then it is not the Holy Spirit speaking to you. It could be a spirit posing as the Holy Spirit, so command it to go from you and refute its lies. Alternatively, it could be your own human spirit talking to you.

The Fire Comes

As already noted, in Luke's account of the Great Commission, Jesus tells the disciple to wait in Jerusalem till they receive the Holy Spirit and are endued with supernatural power:

"And you are witnesses of these things. Behold, I send the Promise of My Father upon you; but tarry in the city of Jerusalem until you are endued with power from on high."

Luke 24:47-48 (KJV)

No one had any idea how it was to happen. Some of them might have recollected the words of John the Baptist when he baptised Jesus at the start of His ministry:

"I indeed baptize you with water; but One mightier than I is coming, whose sandal strap I am not worthy to loose. He will baptize you with the Holy Spirit and fire."

Luke 3:16

Fifty days after the resurrection, on the Day of Pentecost, as the 120 followers including Mary the Mother of Jesus Christ are gathered in the upper room in prayer, the fire of the Holy Spirit indeed falls on them. The impact is mind-blowing:

When the Day of Pentecost had fully come, they were all with one accord in one place. And suddenly there came a sound from heaven, as of a rushing mighty wind, and it filled the whole house where they were sitting. Then there appeared to them divided tongues, as of fire, and one sat upon each of

them. And they were all filled with the Holy Spirit and began
to speak with other tongues, as the Spirit gave them utterance.

Acts 2:1-4

As the tongues of fire fall on them, they begin to speak in languages that are not known to them but are immediately understood by the many visitors from foreign lands who have come for the feast. Then Peter stands up and gives this explosive speech about the death and resurrection of Jesus Christ, ending with a strong declaration of the Lordship of Jesus Christ.

"This Jesus God has raised up, of which we are all witnesses.
Therefore being exalted to the right hand of God, and having
received from the Father the promise of the Holy Spirit, He
poured out this which you now see and hear... Therefore let
all the house of Israel know assuredly that God has made this
Jesus, whom you crucified, both Lord and Christ."

Acts 2:32-33,36

The people are deeply convicted and ask what they should do.

"Repent, and let every one of you be baptized in the name of
Jesus Christ for the remission of sins; and you shall receive the
gift of the Holy Spirit."

Acts 2:38

In his greatest evangelistic sermon, a once timid Peter tells his listeners firstly to *repent* (Greek: *metanoia*), acknowledge your sin and turn away from it or, metaphorically, die to sin.

Secondly, he tells them to *get baptised* (Greek: *baptizo*) which accurately means 'to immerse, dip or plunge'. Notice that *baptizo* is deliberately employed and not the verb to sprinkle (Greek: *rhantizó*); this is because the act of baptism is symbolically an act of being buried after someone has died, and in this case died to sin.

You were buried with Christ when you were baptised. You
were also raised with him to a new life when you were
baptised. You were raised because you believed in the power
of God who raised Christ from death. You were dead because
of the wrong things you had done, and because your lives had

not been made clean. But God gave you life with Christ. He forgave you for all the wrong things you did.

Colossians 2:12-13 (WE)

The third command is that those who repent of their sins and are baptised will receive the promise of the Father which is the Holy Spirit. As stated earlier, the Holy Spirit will help them to fulfil their calling and, by implication, has raised them up from the grave as He did Jesus Christ, for them to walk in the newness of life.

All of these symbols seem to tie in well as 'typology' linking the New Testament with the Old Testament in practice. For example, the Old Testament tabernacle system has a similar procedure:

- *The brazen altar* (Exodus 27:1-8), conspicuously positioned at the outer court of the tabernacle, was a place where Israelites brought their animals to be sacrificed to compensate for their sins. In other words, it was a place of death. In the New Testament this would be repentance, but more importantly, the brazen altar points to the coming Messiah and His death at Calvary.

- *The bronze laver* (Exodus 30:17-21), like baptism, was a basin made from bronze mirror. Because of constant contact with bloody animals, the priest washed his hands and feet to ensure he was spotless before entering into the holy place and the holy of holies. The bronze basin was filled with water for that purpose. This is connected with the plan of salvation as outlined in Peter's Pentecost sermon and links in nicely as a type of baptism,[40] the second step in the process.

- *The holy of holies* was the most sacred and very special place in the tabernacle, entered only by the high priest on the Day of Atonement which happened once a year. This room contained the ark of the Covenant, with its mercy seat, and lighting was provided by the *Shekinah*[41] glory. This was the real deal but only assessible by a very special person, the high priest. This special room represented the presence of God; however, Scripture records:

---

[40] See Acts 2:38

[41] *Shekinah* (Hebrew word): Glory; the divine presence of the Almighty God among His people; see Leviticus 16:2

Jesus called out loud again. Then he died. At that time the thick cloth that hung in the temple was torn into two pieces. It was torn from the top down to the bottom. The earth shook and big rocks broke.

Matthew 27:50-51 (WE)

This means that the ultimate sacrifice has been made and we can now approach boldly the presence of God without hindrance, and this is possible only through the power of the Holy Spirit that Peter advocated on the day of Pentecost.

So, you see how all these tie in: brazen alter = repentance; bronze laver = baptism; Holy Spirit = the holy of holies (the very presence of God).

When Peter preached on the Day of Pentecost, three thousand souls were saved.[42] Signs and wonders followed the apostles and every day more were added to the kingdom.

This small, hastily formed, largely uneducated group became an organised fighting force for the kingdom, preaching fearlessly in the temple and in the marketplace. When the disciples were persecuted by the rulers for preaching Jesus Christ, they were not intimidated, but defended the word and prayed to God for greater boldness to preach and for signs and wonders to follow. Within a very short time, the gospel had spread to Jerusalem, Judea and Samaria, and throngs of Gentiles received Jesus. Led by the Holy Spirit, these followers were unstoppable and advanced the kingdom as far as Rome.

Already the foundations of a vibrant church were in place:[43]

- spreading the apostles' doctrine;
- close fellowship in the breaking of bread and in prayer;
- witnessing wonders and signs everywhere;
- demonstrating compassion and generosity for the needy.

EQUIPPED FOR SERVICE

We must now understand that the Holy Spirit is given for a purpose which is at the very heart of God. Jesus Himself said:

---

[42] See Acts 2:41
[43] See Acts 2:42-47

"But when the Comforter is come, whom I will send unto you from the Father, even the Spirit of truth, which proceedeth from the Father, he shall <u>bear witness of me</u>."

John 15:26 (KJV, emphasis added)

The Holy Spirit has a job to do and that job is to make us fully appreciate what Christ came to do, and then equip and empower us to be witnesses of Jesus Christ to the world, individually and corporately. But we cannot do this in the flesh; we need the convicting power of the Holy Spirit to stir the hearts of unbelievers, for no one can say Jesus is Lord except by the Holy Spirit.[44] That is why Jesus commanded His disciples to wait till they were endued with that power:

"But you shall receive power when the Holy Spirit has come upon you; and you shall be witnesses to Me in Jerusalem, and in all Judea and Samaria, and to the end of the earth."

Acts 1:8

You will see something very interesting in Mark's version of the Great Commission:

And He said to them, "Go into all the world and preach the gospel to every creature. He who believes and is baptized will be saved; but he who does not believe will be condemned. And these signs will follow <u>those who believe</u>: In My name they will cast out demons; they will speak with new tongues; the will take up serpents; and if they drink anything deadly, it will by no means hurt them; they will lay hands on the sick, and they will recover."

Mark 16:15-18 (emphasis added)

Following the teachings of Jesus Christ, power and authority are vested in the hands of the believer rather than in the hierarchy of religious leaders. That means any believer can minister healing and deliverance under the covering of his/her church.

...but you are a chosen people. You are priests to your king. You are a holy nation. You are God's very own people. All

---

[44] See 1 Corinthians 12:3

this is so that you will tell how good he is. He called you out
of darkness into his wonderful light.

1 Peter 2:9 (WE)

In this passage four signs are mentioned that will follow those who believe:

- in Jesus' name they will cast out demons;
- they will speak with new tongues;
- they will have supernatural protection from spiritual and physical attacks;
- they will lay hands on the sick, and the sick will recover.

Where does this power come from? It is given by the Holy Spirit when a new believer comes to Jesus and then receives the Spirit. These four signs were immediately seen in the disciples as they went into the world preaching the word.

And they went out and preached everywhere, the Lord
working with them and confirming the word through the
accompanying signs.

Mark 16:20

This is the Lord's confirmation of His mandate to go out into all the world in the power of the Holy Spirit. Once we receive this power, we must immediately begin to make room for the Spirit to begin His work of transformation, first in our own lives and then in the world around us. To pray for revival is to be revived first as we cannot give what we do not have. John's Gospel clearly laid out those expectations as follows:

- *The Holy Spirit guides believers into all truth.*
  He illumines us when we study the word, opening our eyes to insights, strategies and action plans He has for us.
- *The Holy Spirit convicts the world of sin, righteousness, and judgment.*
  He does not come to condemn people for sin, but to convict, to bring them to a place of repentance by exposing them to their utter inability to deliver themselves from the power of sin.
- *The Holy Spirit empowers the believer to use his authority in Christ over the demonic realm.*
  He reveals the victory believers can have over Satan as a result of the finished work of Calvary. Calvary is a clear demonstration

of the defeat of the "prince of this world" and represents the ultimate victory believers have in Christ Jesus when the Holy Spirit comes to empower and transform us.

- *The Holy Spirit reveals the holiness of God.*
  This helps us to shed our bad habits, change our mindsets and order our lives in a way that is pleasing to Him.

What Next?

Are you ready? Are you excited to hear more? Are you going to run with it?

My brother, my sister, we are called not to be passive hearers but active listeners, so we can take the power within us to change lives. That's why first we need to be filled and baptised with the Holy Spirit.

I am now going to invite you to ask the Holy Spirit to come into your heart and dwell in you. If you have already been baptised with the Holy Spirit, take this time to ask Him to fill you more and give you more strength, especially in areas of vulnerability. You are surrendering your body to be a temple of the Holy Spirit,[45] so do make sure you come to the Father and ask Him to forgive you of all your sins and cleanse you. Do not worry if you have bad habits and addictions that are hard to shake off. The Holy Spirit is here to help you in your struggles. Do not condemn yourself, because you are now in Christ Jesus and have determined to be led by the Holy Spirit.

Are you still worried that you may be led by an evil spirit? I want you to stand on Luke 11:11-13 and believe that your Father will only give you good gifts. Jesus is speaking:

> *"If a son asks for bread from any father among you, will he give him a stone? Or if he asks for a fish, will he give him a serpent instead of a fish? Or if he asks for an egg, will he offer him a scorpion? If you then, being evil, know how to give good gifts to your children, how much more will your heavenly Father give the Holy Spirit to those who ask Him!"*
>
> *Luke 11:11-13*

---

[45] See 1 Corinthians 6:19

As we saw in the Mark 16 passage earlier, and can be found in other places,[46] one of the practical and initial signs of the infilling of the Holy Spirit is speaking in new tongues. That happened to the disciples when the tongues of fire fell on them. When Jesus baptises you in the Holy Spirit, speaking in an unknown language will be one of the first signs that you have received Him. It might not be a human language but it is a special prayer language given by God to you. Jesus said that out of your belly shall flow living waters, speaking of the Holy Spirit.[47]

The Scripture also states:

> *...the person who talks in tongues of a different language does not talk to people, but to God. People do not understand what he says. But he is saying secret things by the Spirit.*
>
> *1 Corinthians 14:2 (WE)*

This is a language of prayer, as the Spirit of the Lord guides us in how we should pray.

Friends, we may be separated by space and time so that I cannot lay hands on you physically. But that does not matter as God is not bound by material things. The anointing of the Lord is upon you as you read these words. Simply accept that the Holy Spirit is with you by faith. And as you invite the Holy Spirit right now with longing, He will take control of you and release your tongue to this new experience.

> *Dear Father, I thank You for giving me Jesus Christ to die in my place and the Holy Spirit to dwell within me. Holy Spirit I welcome You into my life. Come and fill me now. Fill me to overflowing with the evidence of speaking in tongues. Amen!*

If you prayed that prayer with all your heart, just relax and let the Holy Spirit do His part. If you start speaking in tongues, praise the Lord! If you don't yet, don't struggle. The tongues will come in God's good time.

In the next chapter I will be sharing about the ways in which the Holy Spirit both transforms and empowers the believer. I will especially be talking about His fruit and gifts.

---

[46] e.g. Acts 2:38; 2:4; 19:6; 10:45
[47] See John 7:38

CHAPTER FOUR

The Fruit of the Holy Spirit

The measure of a man's character is what he would do if he knew he never would be found out.

Thomas Macaulay

When the mockers on the Day of Pentecost saw the disciples praising God in new tongues, they said they were "drunk with wine". At 9.00 in the morning! But they were not entirely wrong. The disciples were filled with the new wine of the Holy Spirit and were bursting with joy. When was the previous time new wine was mentioned in the Bible? It was Jesus saying that new wine must be put into new wineskins, for if the wineskins are old, the wine will burst the skins.[48]

Think of the new wine as the Holy Spirit pouring His gifts on us so that we can move in healing, signs and wonders, which are the mark of the believer in Christ.[49] Think of the new wineskins as the fruit of the Holy Spirit reflecting a transformed character and a renewed mind in Christ. If we are moving in great healings and miracles but are operating out of our old wineskins, our unrenewed minds, then we will not be able to contain the anointing. We will also be functioning out of our old character, with our old habits and appetites such as pride, anger or lust, which will corrupt the anointing and misrepresent Christ.

Let us explore this a little further. Man is made up of spirit, soul and body. The spirit gives us godly consciousness – this is why every human being intrinsically wants to worship God, a god or anything for that matter – and the spirit is the eternal. The soul gives us self-consciousness which means it is the integral part of our being (who we are). This is the part that Mark 8:36 refers to; it is the only part that has the potential to be eternally lost or rested in Christ in the hereafter. The body gives us

---

[48] See Mark 2:22
[49] See Mark 16:18

material consciousness; it tells us we are hungry, tired and ill, hence Jesus warns:

> *"Don't be afraid of those who kill the body, but are not able to kill the soul. Rather, fear him who is able to destroy both soul and body in Gehenna."*
>
> Matthew 10:28 (WEB)

This aspect of our being is what I term 'animated beef'; as soon as its animation ceases, it becomes useless and the process of decay begins – yet we are invited to glorify God in it as this is the only vessel that contains who we are.[50]

When we accept Christ, the spirit in us reconnects back to God and the work of regeneration begins through the Holy Spirit. As we continue our routine of dying to sin, the soul of the regenerated person becomes subject to the workings of the Holy Spirit which now direct it, and by extension the body becomes subject to divine desire; this is known as being born again.[51]

The moment we are born again, we become a new creation.[52] It is worth remembering that this process starts with the decision to renew our minds, because God created us as beings with free-will, capable of making life-altering decisions.

Renewing Our Minds

How do we renew our minds? Jesus addresses this important question in John 15 in the Garden of Gethsemane discourse:

> *"I am the vine, you are the branches. He who abides in Me, and I in him, bears much fruit; for without Me you can do nothing. If anyone does not abide in Me, he is cast out as a branch and is withered; and they gather them and throw them into the fire, and they are burned. If you abide in Me, and My words abide in you, you will ask what you desire, and it shall be done for you. By this My Father is glorified, that you bear much fruit; so you will be My disciples."*
>
> John 15:5-8

---

[50] See 1 Corinthians 6:12-20
[51] See John 3:3
[52] See 2 Corinthians 5:17

Jesus is the vine, His Father is the vinedresser, we are the branches. The secret of remaining healthy and growing is to *abide* in the vine. This means being organically connected to Jesus and drawing all our sustenance and direction from Him. We draw from the vine primarily from the word, which is Jesus. But we might ask, isn't Jesus in heaven seated at the right hand of the Father? Yes, that is true. But Jesus has given us the word and the Holy Spirit who has made His home on the inside of us. He is the Spirit of truth, who inspired the Bible and who will therefore open up that word for us, to give us fresh insight from heaven for all our needs.

So the branch needs to constantly abide in Jesus and be connected to Him. If not, it withers and is fit for the fire. Saying that we are Christian and not demonstrating a transformed life means that we are Christian in name only. But look what happens when we abide: when we feed on the word, we bear much fruit through the leading of the Holy Spirit, proving ourselves to be followers of Jesus Christ.

The Fruit of the Holy Spirit

In this chapter I want to discuss how we can be more fruitful by allowing the Holy Spirit to cultivate His fruit in us. Paul lists nine fruit of the Holy Spirit:

> *...the fruit of the Spirit is love, joy, peace, longsuffering, kindness, goodness, faithfulness, gentleness, self-control.*
>
> *Galatians 5:22-23*

What is the first thing they remind you of? If you said, "Jesus," I agree with you. Are these not the same traits of Jesus Christ who came to earth as a humble servant and still acts with gentleness and faithfulness and love as a humble servant even in all His glory? They present themselves as soft, but underneath they are steely characteristics.

Notice that Paul talks of "fruit" and not "fruits". This is significant because all the fruit are of the same type. They correspond to the same vine, so they complement and reinforce each other. If, for example, the branch were to produce a fruit called "impatience" and another one called "pride", each would not complement the other, and they would cause each other to lose their shine.

Notice that at the top of the list is love. Love is the quality that produces the life-giving sap to all the other fruit, permeating them with the very essence of God. For God is love.

What is Paul saying? He is saying that a person who displays all the fruit is allowing the Spirit of God to show forth in him the character of Christ and make him a credible witness for Him. He carries the fragrance of life among those who are seeking God, though he may repulse those who are rejecting God:

> *Our lives are a Christ-like fragrance rising up to God. But this fragrance is perceived differently by those who are being saved and by those who are perishing. To those who are perishing, we are a dreadful smell of death and doom. But to those who are being saved, we are a life-giving perfume. And who is adequate for such a task as this?*
>
> *You see, we are not like the many hucksters who preach for personal profit. We preach the word of God with sincerity and with Christ's authority, knowing that God is watching us.*
>
> *2 Corinthians 2:15-17 (NLT)*

In a moment I shall be discussing the fruit in greater depth. But before that I want us to look at the sinful nature we are leaving behind when we come to Christ. The Bible calls the manifestations of that nature "the works of the flesh".

THE WORKS OF THE FLESH

These works are expressions of our former unregenerate nature before we were washed in the blood of Christ. When we came to Jesus Christ, we prayed a general prayer of repentance. Now the Holy Spirit wants us to revisit our obstinate sins and weaknesses to bring home their seriousness so that we can turn away from them and walk a new road.

> *Now the works of the flesh are evident, which are: adultery, fornication, uncleanness, lewdness, idolatry, sorcery, hatred, contentions, jealousies, outbursts of wrath, selfish ambitions, dissensions, heresies, envy, murders, drunkenness, revelries, and the like; of which I tell you beforehand, just as I also told*

you in time past, that those who practice such things will not inherit the kingdom of God.

Galatians 5:19-21

These works of the flesh fall into four categories:

- *sexual sins* (verse 19)
  "adultery, fornication, uncleanness, lewdness";
- *sins associated with false beliefs* (verse 20)
  "idolatry, witchcraft, sorcery, heresies";
- *sin associated with anger and strife* (verse 20)
  "hatred, contentions, jealousies, outbursts of wrath, selfish ambitions, dissensions, envy, murders";
- *sins associated with excesses* (verse 21)
  "drunkenness, revelries, and the like".

Paul warns that those who practise such things will not inherit the kingdom of God.

Do you acknowledge any of them? Anger? Envy? Drinking habit? An addiction?

"Oh, but I only do these things in small doses – like the occasional joint of weed, or idle gossip with family, friends, fellow church members or work colleagues. Nothing so bad in that, is there?"

Dear friend, it starts with the small things that look like human weaknesses. In the end they take control over you. Take backbiting, for instance, which seems innocent enough because nobody gets hurt – ostensibly. But you and your group are feeding that controlling spirit of gossip and strife which seeks to damage lives and reputations through slander – to the extent of breaking up relationships. Our loose tongue can ignite a fire![53]

Or do you secretly engage in an unholy chat or watch adult movies (porn) on the Internet.

"No one's hurt, so what's the big deal? After all, I'm entitled to some entertainment!"

Dear reader, you are feeding the spirit of lust, and before long, your 'innocent' watching is already contaminating your mind and filling you with all kinds of desires. Before long, these desires will want to be put into action.

---

[53] See James 3:1-12

"Well, I do tell a few white lies now and then to get out of sticky situations. I also tend to do the opposite of what my parents ask because I don't like anybody telling me what to do. At any rate, I don't see lying or disobedience in the list."

Ah, but look again. In verse 21 do you see the phrase "...and the like"? That covers lying, cheating, covetousness, disobedience, rebellion and every other sin not mentioned in the list because it would take forever to go through everything. Disobedience, in particular, has very deep roots. A disobedient lifestyle very easily leads to rebellion and the Bible says that rebellion is equivalent to the sin of witchcraft.[54]

All unrighteousness is sin, and there is a sin not leading to death.

1 John 5:17 (WEB)

James the Apostle also issues a severe warning to those of us who tend to take sin lightly and brush it off as only being human.

Temptation comes from our own desires, which entice us and drag us away. These desires give birth to sinful actions. And when sin is allowed to grow, it gives birth to death.

James 1:14-15 (NLT)

These assertions are not intended to condemn or judge; rather they are meant to draw our attention and remind us of the gravity and the consequence of sin in the life of any believer, as well as to help to 'stop the little foxes' on their track from getting through the crack in the fence lest they ruin the whole crop.[55] God does not want us to condemn ourselves either and be weighed down with guilt, but to be thankful that Jesus Christ has already taken that sin on His back. So, do we want to continue in that sin? However long and complicated the journey of faith may seem, God is compassionate and kind and will help us. Please take the first step. Come to a place of repentance and ask God to help you cut this habit off at the root. He will graciously forgive you.[56] Ask the Holy Spirit to help you come out of that bondage and walk a new road.

If that is your desire, then say this prayer with me right now.

---

54 See 1 Samuel 15:23
55 See Song of Solomon 2:15
56 See 1 John 1:9

Father, I acknowledge that I have sinned by my habit(s) of _____. I know that I have sinned against You by my act of rebellion. Please forgive me for wronging You and others I may have hurt, including myself. Holy Spirit, help me to overcome my sins and weaknesses and teach me to walk in holiness. Fill me especially with the fruit of _____. In Jesus' name I pray.

Let us now explore a selection of the fruit of the Spirit.

LOVE

The first and most important fruit is love. As mentioned earlier, love is the sap that enriches all the fruit. God's kind of love is *agape* love. It is different from the human kind of love in that, while human love *philos* or *eros* makes demands on others, God's love is sacrificial and totally giving. Look at how *agape* is expressed in the famous passage on love in 1 Corinthians 13:

> *Though I speak with the tongues of men and of angels, but have not love, I have become sounding brass or a clanging cymbal ... Love suffers long and is kind; love does not envy; love does not parade itself, is not puffed up; does not behave rudely, does not seek its own, is not provoked, thinks no evil; does not rejoice in iniquity, but rejoices in the truth; bears all things, believes all things, hopes all things, endures all things. Love never fails.*
>
> *1 Corinthians 13:1,4-8*

Take a look at the above text and see how many of the other fruit are mentioned there or alluded to: long-suffering, kindness, goodness, faithfulness, gentleness, joy, self-control – almost all of them. And though "peace" is not directly mentioned, we can assume that great peace comes upon the one who operates in love.

When we have love we seek the highest good of our fellowman and are not motivated by self-interest. No one can love in that fashion except through the Holy Spirit filling us with God's compassion.

When a rich young ruler came to Jesus asking how he should gain eternal life, Jesus told him to keep the commandments. But when the young man said he had observed all the commandments from young, Jesus replied:

"If you want to be perfect, go, sell what you have and give to the poor, and you will have treasure in heaven; and come, follow Me."

Matthew 16:19-22

You see, the young man was operating out of a legalistic perspective of the commandments, but the spirit was not quite there. His heart was empty because he lacked God's extravagant love. Sadly, he was unable to release all his possessions and Jesus knew that they were controlling him. Giving everything to the poor and following Jesus would have given him the freedom to enter into the dimension of God's superabundance. It would also point the way to becoming perfect, that is, complete in everything, lacking nothing. The point also to remember is this: it is possible to give gifts without necessarily loving the recipient of that gift but it almost impossible to love without giving. This is why John 3:16 tells us that the love of God for the world preceded His gift to it.

PEACE

Before Jesus went to the cross, He released His peace on His disciples.

"Peace I leave with you, My peace I give to you; not as the world gives do I give to you. Let not your heart be troubled, neither let it be afraid."

John 14:27

The Greek word for 'peace' is generally *eirene,* which is close in meaning to the Hebrew word *shalom.* It means freedom, not just from unrest, but freedom to be everything that promotes our highest good, physically, spiritually, materially, mentally and emotionally. The peace that Jesus gives is not the fleeting peace the world gives. It is a stable, lasting peace which can say, "Peace, be still!" in the midst of storms. This kind of peace is not the absence of trouble but the state of the believer's mind in troubled times.

We already have peace with God and with our fellowman because Jesus Christ has broken down every wall of separation.[57] And as we fix our thoughts on Him, trusting Him, He will continue to keep our mind in perfect peace.[58]

---

[57] See Ephesians 2:14
[58] See Isaiah 26:3

Since God's peace transcends earthly matters, we can bring our cares and anxieties before the Lord and rest confidently in the peace of God to guard our hearts and minds.

> *Be anxious for nothing, but in everything by prayer and supplication, with thanksgiving, let your requests be made known to God; and the peace of God, which surpasses all understanding, will guard your hearts and minds through Christ Jesus.*
>
> *Philippians 4:6-7*

JOY

The very fact that we have been not only saved and delivered, but seated in the heavenly places with Jesus Christ, will make us want to shout for joy. Surely coming into such a great salvation just through our confession of Jesus is more than we could ever ask or imagine!

> *But God, who is rich in mercy, because of His great love with which He loved us, even when we were dead in trespasses, made us alive together with Christ (by grace you have been saved), and raised us up together, and made us sit together in the heavenly places in Christ Jesus...*
>
> *Ephesians 2:4-6*

Like peace, our joy is deep-seated. It is not dictated to us by circumstances, but we can draw from the Holy Spirit when we are in the toughest of situations. The joy of the *Lord* is our strength, not the joy of the *town*.

Consider Nehemiah and his team building the wall of Jerusalem regardless of the severe challenges: the heat, the debris, the squalor, their enemies taunting them, the need for continuous vigilance against attack, while at the same time working feverishly round the clock.[59] They overcame and completed the wall in record time – fifty-two days – because of that supernatural infusion of joy.

LONG-SUFFERING

The Greek word *makrothumia*, literally 'long-temper', can be translated into 'long-suffering' or 'patience'. James tells us to consider it

---

[59] Read the whole story in the Book of Nehemiah

all joy when we fall into trials because "the testing of your faith produces patience. But let patience have its perfect work, that you may be perfect and complete, lacking nothing."[60]

So, patience is a stepping stone to our being made complete and perfect.

In this digital age when we expect everything to happen at the click of a mouse, patience is a rare quality. It helps us put up with delays, traffic jams, inconvenience and troublesome people without complaining or getting unduly upset.

But more than the day-to-day hassles, patience prepares us for long periods of drought where prayers are yet to be answered and we are often thrust into a limbo of uncertainty. Here is that waiting period where much patience is called for. Here is the season of the greatest potential growth and breakthrough:

> *But they that wait upon the LORD shall renew their strength;*
> *they shall mount up with wings as eagles; they shall run, and*
> *not be weary; and they shall walk, and not faint.*
>
> *Isaiah 40:31 (KJV)*

Jesus told His disciples, "By your patience possess your soul."[61] This came at the brink of Jesus going to the cross and warning them of the persecution that was to come. How can our patience possess our soul? By being intentional and expectant during our wait. By telling ourselves to look beyond the pain and heartache to God's promises and expect a new day.

If you have received a prophetic word which is slow in coming to pass, do not be discouraged. Remember that without tribulation there will be no patience. In effect, trial is the forerunner of patience, so instead of praying for patience, pray for trials; they are what will determine your patience. The faith that has not been tested cannot be trusted. Write it down. Visit it often to keep it fresh on your mind:

> *Write the vision*
> *And make it plain on tablets,*
> *That he may run who reads it.*
> *For the vision is yet for an appointed time;*

---

[60] James 1:3-4
[61] Luke 21:19

But at the end it will speak, and it will not lie.
Though it tarries, wait for it;
Because it will surely come,
It will not tarry.

Habakkuk 2:2-3

FAITHFULNESS

"Faithfulness" and "faith" are derived from the same Greek word, *pistis*. As "faith", *pistis* refer to trusting in what the Bible says about God: His existence, His word and His promises, and His very disposition. As "faithfulness", *pistis* can be interpreted as the quality of trustworthiness, steadfastness, constancy, or allegiance.

We are faithful by being trustworthy in whatever we have been called to do – from the little things to the great. We begin on the premise that God entrusts us to be stewards of His vineyard and take good care of it until He returns.[62]

I want to draw your attention to this verse in the Book of Philippians:

Not that I seek the gift, but I seek the profit that accumulates
to your account.

Philippians 4:17 (NASB)

You see, every child of God has a divine account with God, in which there is a divine balance sheet to be attended to in the same way our banking system operates. From time to time, we should therefore make a faithful inventory, taking stock of the content of our own account. Where there are deficits, we should correct them, and where there are credits, we should build on them.

Faithful inventory will show the condition of our service to God: how much we have sown into cultivating our relationship with Him, enriching our prayer lives and drawing revelation from the word. All of these translate into credits accumulating in our heavenly account. They add up to continuous investments we make in terms of *time, talent* and *treasure*. Consider the amount of time we spend sharing the good news of Jesus to others, showing care and kindness in the name of the Lord, and how we use our time, resources and talents to advance the kingdom of heaven.

---

[62] See Matthew 25:14-25

For the Son of Man will come in the glory of His Father with His angels, and then He will reward each according to his works.

Matthew 16:27 (KJV)

Let us be counted worthy when the Lord of the harvest calls us as stewards to give an account of our lives. What joy when He pats us on the back and says:

"'Well done, good and faithful servant; you were faithful over a few things, I will make you ruler over many things. Enter into the joy of your lord.'"

Matthew 25:21

GENTLENESS

Gentleness is also translated as "meekness"[63]. But it's not a weakness; it's a strength. It's that quality of being kind to one another, tenderhearted, forgiving one another, even as God in Christ forgave us.[64]

Gentleness can be described as *'power under control'* because I am yielding my will to the Holy Spirit. I am tempted to defend my point in a heated argument or show the other person up for what they really are – a noise bag! – but I choose to bring it up at another place, another time. And when I do, I convey it in a spirit of genuine gentleness, not one that is laced with sarcasm. I want to uphold the person's rights and dignity to be heard – but on amicable terms. When I choose to move in the spirit of gentleness, I place my strength under God's mighty hand, and then it becomes a powerful tool.

Gentleness is most often displayed by our affirming words. We have the choice of speaking words of life or death over people or situations.[65] Let us speak life to distressing situations and offer comfort because of our gentle words.

And, if we have to confront a person because of their public sin or some other issue, let us do so in a spirit of gentleness. Paul tells us:

---

[63] e.g. AMP
[64] See Ephesians 4:32
[65] See Proverbs 18:21

74

...if a man is caught in any transgression, you who are spiritual should restore such a one in the spirit of meekness, watching yourselves, lest you also be tempted.

Galatians 6:1-2 (MEV)

SELF-CONTROL

The last characteristic listed among the fruit is self-control, or temperance. This is, of course, the ability to control one's feelings and emotions. It involves exercising discipline and restraint when we want to give in to ungodly desires and fleshly lusts such as rage, sexual appetites (including pornography), gossip, slander, lying, cheating and rebellion. It means recognising the enemy's fear tactics that would make us want to cave in and retreat. It also means alertness when we are tempted to allow our emotions to blind us to the actual move of God in our lives.

For the weapons of our warfare are not carnal but mighty in God for pulling down strongholds.

2 Corinthians 10:4

Water can be a deadly foe when it overflows the river and floods the land, causing devastation and loss of life. But when that watercourse is directed towards a dam and harnessed for hydroelectric power, or used for irrigating farmland, then it can be used for much good.

We have an enemy who is very crafty and will use our vulnerabilities, especially our emotions, to destabilise and derail us. He will speak into our circumstances to cause fear, confusion, intimidation and anger. This can sometimes overwhelm us and blind us to the truth that God is with us working with and on behalf of us, that He has never left us nor forsaken us, that all our prayers have been heard.

Yes, our emotions are our greatest vulnerability. But when we learn to channel them like the river, they can be our greatest asset. The Lord wants to use our emotions as a catalyst to direct our energies to taking cities and nations for Him, pushing back the powers of darkness, repenting for the wickedness of our society. But first we must determine to surrender all our emotions to the Lord to be sanctified for His use. We must align our mind, our will and our emotions to His larger purposes. I hope these words strengthen you whatever you are going through right now:

He who is slow to anger is better than the mighty,
And he who rules his spirit than he who takes a city.

Proverbs 16:32

My brother, my sister, will you arise with me out of every enemy attack? Go to your prayer closet or your prayer group, and ask the Lord to take control over the situation. Then launch your counterattack against your real enemy: the devil. Let us arise and gird up the loins of our minds to put confusion in the enemy camp![66]

---

[66] See Job 3:38

CHAPTER FIVE

The Gifts of the Holy Spirit

Many saints cannot distinguish inspiration from emotion.
Actually these two can be defined readily. Emotion always
enters from man's outside, whereas inspiration originates with
the Holy Spirit in man's spirit.

Watchman Nee[67]

From the Day of Pentecost, the early church spread rapidly because the good news was preached, with signs and wonders following. Extraordinary healings were taking place such as Peter's shadow being cast upon the sick and healing them, and Paul's handkerchiefs being used to transfer the anointing;[68] the dead were raised and demons were cast out.[69] People who saw the supernatural power of God were convicted of sin and lives were transformed. Jesus had said that we would do greater works than He did,[70] and this was happening before their very eyes.

Today there are many scoffers, including traditionally-minded churchgoers, who say that Pentecost was a one-time event and cannot be replicated in our day. They are misinformed and are limiting the enduring work of the Holy Spirit. If they would only open their spiritual eyes beyond the news in the mainstream media, they would see that there has been a mighty move of God in the twentieth century, touching nations. The revivals that broke out in Wales in 1904, in Azusa Street, Los Angeles in 1908, in Canada, in Argentina, in Korea and in many other parts of the world over the past hundred years are very well documented. The most compelling feature of these revivals has been a deep conviction of sin and a longing to know Jesus.

---

[67] Quoted from Shawn Jones, *Answer Me!* (Morrisville, North Carolina: *Lulu.com*, 2017),122.
[68] See Acts 5:15-16; 19:12
[69] See Acts 9:36-42; 16:16-19
[70] See John 14:12

God is not a man that He should lie. What He says in His word, He will watch over to perform.[71] And what Peter declared from the Book of Joel is surely about to break forth in our day:

> *"'And it shall come to pass in the last days, says God,*
> *That I will pour out of My Spirit on all flesh;*
> *Your sons and your daughters shall prophesy,*
> *Your young men shall see visions,*
> *Your old men shall dream dreams.*
> *And on My menservants and on My maidservants*
> *I will pour out My Spirit in those days;*
> *And they shall prophesy.'"*
>
> *Acts 2:17-18*

Notice that this prophecy is for us "in the last days" and all the signs point to the soon coming of Christ in His glory. Let us not be passive spectators because God wants us to participate in this greatest outpouring of the Holy Spirit in our history. Let us expect and prepare ourselves for revival – in our village, town, city, nation, region and indeed in the nations of the world.

That is why understanding and moving in the gifts of the Holy Spirit is so crucial to our being equipped for the mission of God on earth. Please be excited about all these wonderful gifts of God to us, and more importantly, be expectant and ask the Holy Spirit to breathe upon you and release the gifts He has prepared for you.

The Gifts of the Holy Spirit

> *Now concerning spiritual gifts, brethren, I do not want you to be ignorant:*
>
> *There are diversities of gifts, but the same Spirit. There are differences of ministries, but the same Lord. And there are diversities of activities, but it is the same God who works all in all. But the manifestation of the Spirit is given to each one for the profit of all: for to one is given the word of wisdom through the Spirit, to another the word of knowledge through the same Spirit, to another faith by the same Spirit, to another gifts of healings by the same Spirit, to another the working of*

---

[71] See Jeremiah 1:12

miracles, to another prophecy, to another discerning of spirits, to another different kinds of tongues, to another the interpretation of tongues. But one and the same Spirit works all these things, distributing to each one individually as He wills.

1 Corinthians 12:1,4-11

There are different kinds of gifts but the same Holy Spirit who gives to each individual the gifts He sees fit. These gifts are not for our personal consumption or for showing off, but are tools the Holy Spirit manifests in us for the benefit of people so that God will be glorified.

There are altogether nine gifts which fall into three categories of three:

- First there are the *revelatory* gifts, which provide supernatural insight into things: words of wisdom, words of knowledge and the discerning of spirits.
- Next are the *power* gifts, which demonstrate the power of Almighty God: faith, healings and miracles.
- Finally, there are the *utterance* gifts, which are supernaturally charged words: tongues, interpretation of tongues and prophecy.

Here is how they operate through the Holy Spirit.

The Revelatory Gifts

WISDOM

Generally, most people, whether believers or not, have some form of intrinsic wisdom, the ability to distinguish between things. However, divine wisdom is only bestowed on a regenerated person as part of the gift of the Holy Spirit; that is when God allows unusual insight to override our natural predisposition, and on such occasion the result will be evident to all around.

Paul the Apostle was a man who operated in the shadow of divine wisdom. For example, in Acts 17:16-34 we find him in the midst of the Athenians on Mars Hill with their multiple gods. Paul, however, used their own imaginations (the alter dedicated to an unknown god) to bring the message of the saving grace of God through Christ to them in a very powerful way, such that they narrowly escaped being convicted and extended a speaking invite to him for another date.

KNOWLEDGE

The word of knowledge, as one of the gifts of the Spirit, is a divine insight into some privileged information that could not have intuitively been known without the help of the Holy Spirit. These words of knowledge can be very precise, to the point of naming names. In Acts 5:1-11, Ananias and Sapphira's lies were brought to light through this means. The couple sold their land as others were doing but they kept a part of it to themselves and lied about it. God revealed to Peter their treachery and as a result the couple paid the supreme price.

Some time ago I was experiencing a very challenging time in my family. A friend I have known for many years and who resides in another country sent me a text message recounting to me the very situation I was in. His revelation was on point and I could not deny it but simply admitted it and requested that he should continue to hold me and my family in prayers. Undoubtedly, this friend of mine had a very precise piece of exposé that he could not perchance have known except somebody had told him.

These two gifts are in some ways linked. The word of wisdom guards us by helping us apply the word of knowledge which we have been privileged to receive, and thus serves as a guide into the divine purpose for our lives. Do not, therefore, act independently, but as far as possible, wait for the Holy Spirit to give you the word of wisdom *and* knowledge before anything else. Otherwise, the act of simple disobedience might land you in big trouble that you are unable to handle.

DISCERNING OF SPIRITS

The discerning of spirits is different from general discernment, which is the ability to judge or sense things through your own natural ability. The discerning of spirits involves seeing into the spirit realm to know whether the spirits are of God or from the devil, and which kind of spirits are operating. This gift is vital for all believers especially those involved in ministry; it is a tool for engaging in spiritual warfare.

In Acts 16, Paul and Silas were preaching in Philippi. Their meetings were interrupted by a slave girl who practised fortune-telling for her owners. She would follow Paul and Silas around, crying:

"These men are the servants of the Most High God, who proclaim to us the way of salvation."

Acts 16:17

However, this gift of spiritual discernment came in play. Paul could instantaneously distinguish between the evil spirit in operation and the Holy Spirit working with them, so he commanded it to come out of her. What the girl was saying was true, but Paul was able to discern the spirit of divination and did not need an evil spirit to endorse their ministry.

When we are praying for someone who is oppressed or possessed, we can ask the Holy Spirit to reveal the spirit that is behind the person so we can deal with it accordingly. The gift of the discerning of spirits is key, especially for those engaged in praying for cities and nations, as it will help in differentiating evil spirits controlling those territories from the Holy Spirit and help you to strategise correctly. The control of such spirits can be manifest in various types of sin prevailing in those areas, such as idolatry, prostitution, organised crime, drug peddling, and much prayer and intercession is needed to confront those spirits.

Ask the Holy Spirit to give you the gift of discerning of spirits so that you can pray more effectively for your community, your school or workplace, even for different members of your family.

The Power Gifts

FAITH, HEALINGS AND MIRACLES

These gifts also reinforce one another. You must have faith to begin with to move in healings, and even greater faith to see miracles in demonstration of God's creative power.

The gift of faith is greater than a general faith to believe for healing. The gift of faith is a sudden surge of faith to believe for a miracle in a particular circumstance. It is released by the Holy Spirit whenever, wherever and to whomever He wishes. This could happen at a healing service saturated with the presence of God with an anointed servant of God who has the gifts of healing. Notice that there are *gifts* of healing as the Holy Spirit desires. The speaker may have a general gift of healing or a specific healing for certain conditions.

Collective faith can also be generated by the congregation as they come full of faith and expectancy as expressed in their worship. This is very important for the right atmosphere for miracles to happen.

The Utterance Gifts

TONGUES

The gifts of speaking in tongues and the interpretation of tongues are perhaps the most controversial of all the gifts because there are many views regarding what is meant by "tongues" and whether the gifts are still active today. Many objections to the use of tongues come from traditional churches, as well as believers who do not see the relevance of such gifts in our time.

The best way to counter these objections is the word.

- *Objection 1: Tongues were for Pentecost only*
  But Jesus Himself said that tongues, among the other gifts, are one of the signs of the believer:

  And these signs will follow those who believe: In My name they will cast out demons; they will speak with new tongues; they will take up serpents; and if they drink anything deadly, it will by no means hurt them; they will lay hands on the sick, and they will recover.

  Mark 16:17-18 (emphasis added)

- *Objection 2: Public opinion*
  Many people feel uncomfortable speaking aloud in tongues for fear of being laughed at for talking gibberish. But God uses the "foolish" and "weak" things to shame the wise and mighty.

  But God has chosen the foolish things of the world to put to shame the wise, and God has chosen the weak things of the world to put to shame the things which are mighty...

  1 Corinthians 1:27

  Speaking in tongues is therefore a real test of our faith. It is teaching us to overcome the fear of man and our own doubts, especially when we don't know what we are praying. It releases us to become vulnerable before our God and people, and it also empowers us in our prayers.

  For if I pray in a tongue, my spirit prays, but my understanding is unfruitful...

  1 Corinthians 14:14

- *Objection 3: Fake tongues*

  Within denominations themselves, there is heated debate about which tongues are genuine and which are fake and made up by the speaker. Those who value only "genuine tongues" point to the Day of Pentecost, when the disciples began speaking in tongues which, though unknown to them, were understood by the visitors to Jerusalem from other parts of Asia. So here we have tongues which are unknown to the speakers but known to the wider audience. This group believes that our tongues should be recognisable in a known language to be genuine.

  But look at what the word of God says:

Though I speak with the tongues of men and <u>of angels</u>...

1 Corinthians 13:1 (emphasis added)

This means that in addition to the "tongues of men" i.e. known languages, there is such a thing as "tongues of angels". So our heavenly language, not known to man, is a tongue of angels. Who understands this heavenly language?

For he who speaks in a tongue does not speak to men but to God, for no one understands him; however, in the spirit he speaks mysteries.

1 Corinthians 14:2

Do not allow anyone to talk you out of using this special heavenly language given to you by the Holy Spirit. You are walking by faith and not by sight as you choose to honour God and communicate in your special language.

WHAT ARE THE BENEFITS OF TONGUES?

Tongues are generally the first evidence that we are filled with the Holy Spirit. Throughout the Book of Acts, we plainly see that all who were baptised in the Holy Spirit almost immediately started speaking in tongues. Once you understand the tremendous benefits of speaking in tongues, you will cease to be concerned about all the objections from the worldly wise.

You will want the benefits:

- *a richer prayer life*

As we develop the gift of speaking and singing in tongues, we find we have a variety of tongues for different occasions: praise tongues, intercessory tongues, warfare tongues.

When you have prayed all you can in your own understanding, let the Spirit of God take over and give you the perfect prayer in His language.

- *stronger faith*[72]

   Since we are being obedient to God by believing and trusting in His word, we are building ourselves up in our most holy faith by praying in the Spirit.

- *flow of other gifts*

   As you speak in tongues, the flow of the Spirit makes it easier to move into any of the other gifts: word of knowledge, word of wisdom, prophecy, healings or greater faith to believe in miracles.

- *refreshing and rest*[73]

   Tongues usher in the stronger presence of God. There is peace. He will refresh you and give you His rest.

- *rivers of living water*[74]

   Tongues enable the Holy Spirit to fill you more and more. When you have the Holy Spirit in full to overflowing, you are releasing life and abundance to all those around you.

INTERPRETATION OF TONGUES

Sometimes in a church or fellowship meeting filled with believers, in the midst of the worship, one speaker may break out in tongues in a loud voice. Then there is a pause and another member may give the interpretation of it in a language known to the group. This happens when God wants to address the body corporately rather than individually. This is called the interpretation of tongues.

> *If there is no interpretation, then the one who spoke should be silent and not continue in tongues.*
>
> 1 Corinthians 14:27-28

---

[72] See Jude 20
[73] See Isaiah 28:12
[74] See John 7:37-39

I need to explain the difference between tongues and interpretation of tongues. First, there are personal tongues, which is the heavenly prayer language given to you by the Holy Spirit. You speak these tongues in a private setting or even together with believers at a prayer meeting. These are the tongues Paul refers to when he says:

> *I wish you all spoke with tongues...*
>
> *1 Corinthians 14:5*

Then there are tongues which require interpretation because they are spoken loudly and with authority at a public meeting. Both types of tongues are mentioned in the scripture below:

> *I wish you all spoke with tongues [i.e. tongues without interpretation], but even more that you prophesied; for he who prophesies is greater than he who speaks with tongues, unless indeed he interprets [i.e. tongues with interpretation], that the church may receive edification.*
>
> *1 Corinthians 14:5*

The first mention of tongues refers to tongues without interpretation and the second to tongues with interpretation. Paul is saying that if tongues are released in public, he wishes that there would be interpretation so that all present can edified or built up.

Notice that in the above passage Paul also says that prophecy is greater than tongues (personal tongues) unless there is interpretation. This means that the interpretation of tongues is almost on par with the gift of prophecy.

PROPHECY

Of all the gifts of the Holy Spirit, Paul urges us to desire the gift of prophecy because "he who prophesies speaks edification and exhortation and comfort to men"[75].

The reason that prophecy is higher than any other gift is because it edifies the church. This means that prophecy is higher than personal tongues which edify just the individual, but it is at the same level as the interpretation of tongues which also edifies the whole body.

Prophecy not only edifies; it also seeks to exhort and comfort.

---

[75] 1 Corinthians 14:3

To exhort is to encourage or lift the church up. For example, a speaker could exhort the church to be a voice in the marketplace and pursue holiness, especially when the members are facing great discouragement.

Comfort is closely related to exhortation. It eases a person's feelings of grief or distress. A prophetic word that encourages and uplifts will also comfort the hearers in the midst of the challenges they are going through.

All three – edification, exhortation and comfort – release supernatural strength to the hearers. They may need that prophetic word to hold on to their core values in the midst of pressures from society to compromise.

What is the conclusion then? Let's do what Paul does and use tongues, interpretation of tongues and prophecy in the appropriate settings:

> *I will pray with the spirit, and I will also pray with the understanding. I will sing with the spirit, and I will also sing with the understanding ... I thank my God I speak with tongues more than you all; yet in the church I would rather speak five words with my understanding, that I may teach others also, than ten thousand words in a tongue.*
>
> *1 Corinthians 14:15;18-19*

CHAPTER SIX

Faith to Live By

Faith is like radar that sees through the fog – the reality of things at a distance that the human eye cannot see.

Corrie Ten Boom

We need not only the faith to see miracles but a sustaining, abiding kind of faith to see us through all the twists and turns of life. What is this kind of faith and how do we acquire it? In this chapter I will attempt to explore the biblical interpretation of faith and also how we can appropriate it.

Let us begin with the biblical definition of faith.

Now <u>faith</u> is the <u>substance</u> of things hoped for, the <u>evidence</u> of things not seen

Hebrews 11:1 (emphasis added)

Let us unpack the three underlined keywords: *faith, substance* and *evidence.*

First, we recognise that biblical faith (*pistis* in Greek), while linked to hope, is different from hope. While hope is generally experienced in the emotions (*psuche* in Greek), faith springs from the heart (*kardia* in Greek). Kardia is the seat and centre of human life including moral decisions. Therefore, we can say that faith is deeper-rooted than hope.

Secondly, faith is not blind faith, believing in fiction or wishful thinking. It is based on substance. The Greek word for "substance" here is *hupostasis,* which means 'placing or setting under a substructure or foundation', in other words, 'an undergirding'. Think of faith as a sturdy bridge which is supported underneath by strong steel undergirding. That's how solid faith is. It is this unwavering support that gives us the assurance or confidence that the thing we have hoped and prayed for will come to pass.

Third, the word "evidence" comes from the Greek word *elengchos,* meaning 'proof' or 'that by which a thing is proved or tested' or 'a conviction'. Now, remember that we are looking at the invisible realm of thoughts and convictions, so what solid evidence can that produce? The solid evidence is the word of God which is as solid as a rock. The word reveals the nature of God and all His works, His laws and His promises, including the specific promise He has given in our situation.

How Faith Grows

Faith begins as mustard seed faith. We are going to examine this concept of mustard seed faith in the Bible narrative about the boy with epilepsy; from here we can draw out some important principles about faith and the conditions in which it operates.

THE BOY WITH EPILEPSY

Jesus, Peter, James and John had just returned from the Mountain of Transfiguration[76] to the other disciples. They saw a large crowd surrounding them and some teachers of religious law arguing with them. On seeing Jesus, the crowd were overwhelmed with awe and ran to greet Him.

> *Then one of the crowd answered and said, "Teacher, I brought You my son, who has a mute spirit. And wherever it seizes him, it throws him down; he foams at the mouth, gnashes his teeth, and becomes rigid. So I spoke to Your disciples, that they should cast it out, but they could not."*
>
> *He answered him and said, "O <u>faithless generation</u>, how long shall I be with you? How long shall I bear with you? Bring him to Me." Then they brought him to Him. And when he saw Him, immediately the spirit convulsed him, and he fell on the ground and wallowed, foaming at the mouth.*
>
> *So He asked his father, "How long has this been happening to him?"*

---

[76] The Mountain of Transfiguration: the mount upon which Jesus was transformed along with historic figures; see Matthew 17:1-9, Mark 9:2-13 and Luke 9:28-36

And he said, "From childhood. And often he has thrown him both into the fire and into the water to destroy him. But if You can do anything, have compassion on us and help us."

Jesus said to him, "If you can believe, <u>all things are possible to him who believes</u>."

Immediately the father of the child cried out and said with tears, "Lord, I believe; help my unbelief!"

When Jesus saw that the people came running together, He rebuked the unclean spirit, saying to it, "Deaf and dumb spirit, I command you, come out of him and enter him no more!" Then the spirit cried out, convulsed him greatly, and came out of him. And he became as one dead, so that many said, "He is dead." But Jesus took him by the hand and lifted him up, and he arose.

And when He had come into the house, His disciples asked Him privately, "Why could we not cast it out?"

So He said to them, "<u>This kind can come out by nothing but prayer and fasting</u>."

Mark 9:17-29 (emphasis added)

So, the disciples were confronted with their first great challenge. They had already been trained by Jesus, sent out to the villages with power over unclean spirits, and had come back with glowing reports of healing and deliverance.[77] Now they were unable to cast out this stubborn spirit. What a let-down! What had gone wrong?

The first indication of where they had gone wrong was Jesus' rebuke, calling them a "faithless generation"[78]. What had caused their loss of faith?

Could the clue be the fearful descriptions of the evil spirit's manifestations, causing the boy to foam at the mouth, gnash his teeth, become rigid, convulsing him and throwing him into the fire and water to destroy him? Could all these violent displays in the midst of a troubled father and crowd have so alarmed the disciples that their faith was shaken? Could it also have been the confusion caused by the teachers of

---

[77] See Mark 6:7-13
[78] verse 19

religious law arguing with them? Could the circumstances have been so overwhelming, their faith buckled and unbelief took over?

Yes to all of that. Certainly, the disciples had been thrown off guard by the drama. But could the answer also be found in the spiritual condition of the disciples? Look further down the chapter:

> *Then He came to Capernaum. And when He was in the house He asked them, "What was it you disputed among yourselves on the road?" But they kept silent, for on the road they had disputed among themselves who would be the greatest.*
>
> *Mark 9:33-34*

We see now that the spirit of strife and competition had been brewing in them for quite a while. Even after the epileptic boy miracle, their attention was still caught up with which of them would be the greatest. Since there was division among them and their minds were distracted, they were unable to take authority over the demonic realm.

In Matthew's version of the same episode here is Jesus' analysis:

> *Then the disciples came to Jesus privately and said, "Why could we not cast it out?"*
>
> *So Jesus said to them, "Because of your unbelief; for assuredly, I say to you, if you have faith as a mustard seed, you will say to this mountain, 'Move from here to there,' and it will move; and nothing will be impossible for you."*
>
> *Matthew 17:19-20*

Doubt and unbelief would certainly have added to the difficulty of operating in miracles. Even Jesus found His hometown Nazareth hard ground and was not able to perform many miracles there,[79] while He performed some of His greatest miracles in Capernaum because of their faith.[80]

Another compelling reason was Jesus' ability to discern the spiritual forces at work and His terse statement, "This kind can come out by nothing but prayer and fasting."[81] By this, I do not think Jesus was referring to ritualistic fasting but the kind of fasting that pleases the

---

[79] See Mark 6:5
[80] See Matthew 11:23-24
[81] See Mark 9:29

Lord.[82] Only a lifestyle disciplined by this type of fasting could produce wholeness, insight and effectiveness in ministry:

The LORD will guide you continually,
And satisfy your soul in drought,
And strengthen your bones;
You shall be like a watered garden,
And like a spring of water, whose waters do not fail.

Isaiah 58:11

So what have we established about faith so far?

- The motives of the ministry team are important.
- Physical circumstances can be distracting and throw off faith.
- Prayer and fasting are needed in stubborn cases.
- Even mustard seed faith can move mountains.

I want you to consider further astounding statements Jesus makes about faith:

"If you can believe, all things are possible to him who believes."

Mark 9:23

"With men this is impossible, but with God all things are possible."

Matthew 19:26

And Jesus answering saith unto them, Have faith of God.

Mark 11:22 (KJV)

The last statement could be interpreted as, "Have the faith of God or God's kind of faith."

MUSTARD SEED FAITH

Jesus says that even 'mustard seed faith' can move mountains or remove obstructions to our breakthrough. We know that the mustard seed will grow into an enormous tree. But let us look beyond that to the word "seed". Genesis 1:21 says that everything that God created is according to its own kind. Therefore, the seed faith that God deposits in your heart is according to His nature, which is full of radical faith and

---

[82] See Isaiah 58:3-12

creative ideas. So when we say, "Have faith in God," "God's kind of faith," or, "With God all things are possible," what we are really saying is that when we have God's faith, we are endued with a radically different kind of faith from that of the world.

FAITH TO DECLARE

Jesus not only talks about mustard seed faith, He talks about making faith-filled declarations:

> *"For assuredly, I say to you, whoever says to this mountain, 'Be removed and be cast into the sea,' and does not doubt in his heart, but believes that those things he says will be done, he will have whatever he says."*
>
> Mark 11:23

> *"...if you have faith as a mustard seed, you will say to this mountain, 'Move from here to there,' and it will move; and nothing will be impossible for you."*
>
> Matthew 17:20

> *"If you had faith even as small as a mustard seed, you could say to this mulberry tree, 'May you be uprooted and be planted in the sea,' and it would obey you!"*
>
> Luke 17:6

Jesus says to speak to the mountain of difficulty or defeat. The words that we release are spirit and life and we know that death and life are in the power of the tongue.[83] Just as God created the world by the power of His words – "Let there be ... and there was"[84] – so also do we, as spiritual sons of Abraham, have the power to call things that are not into being according to His word:

> *Therefore, the promise comes by faith, so that it may be by grace and may be guaranteed to all Abraham's offspring—not only to those who are of the law but also to <u>those who have the faith of Abraham</u>. He is the father of us all. As it is written: "I have made you a father of many nations." He is our father*

---

[83] See John 6:63; Proverbs 18:21
[84] See Genesis 1:3-26

in the sight of God, in whom he believed—the God who gives life to the dead and calls into <u>being things that were not</u>.

Romans 4:16-17 (NIV, emphasis added)

There is a tremendous power in this spiritual principle: *we shape our own reality by the words which we speak.*

By faith we understand that the entire universe was formed at God's command, that what we now see did not come from anything that can be seen.

Hebrews 11:4 (NLT)

God spoke and the universe came into being. Similarly, we can speak words of faith into the atmosphere and see them change circumstances and create new life.

Remember that your salvation came through believing Jesus is Lord and speaking it out aloud. The faith in your heart was translated into your faith-filled confession.

So how do we acquire faith?

FAITH COMES BY HEARING

So, then faith comes by hearing, and hearing by the word of God.

Romans 10:17

Belief based on hearing the word of God ignites faith. The Roman centurion whose servant was ill, the Canaanite woman whose daughter was demon-possessed, the woman with an issue of blood did not have written bibles like we do. It was through word of mouth. They heard the news of Jesus, heard about His miracles, believed that He was the Son of David and, based on that, acted on their faith to reach out to Him.

When news arrived that this Preacher was near Jericho, blind Bartimaeus knew that this was his moment. He could not see, but he could hear and he had good lungs. So he shouted, "Jesus, Son of David, have mercy on me!" And when they told him to be quiet, he shouted all the more.[85] That is the 'now' kind of faith that jumps to action by recognising the solution.

This is why preaching God's word is very crucial in every generation including the twenty-first century. By this I do not mean motivational

---

[85] See Mark 10:46-52

speaking but words – and not just any words but the word of God; it informs, conforms and transforms our minds through the inspiration of the Holy Spirit.

FAITH GROWS BY READING THE WORD

Through the word we know the nature of God, that His plans for us are good,[86] that He is entirely trustworthy and can be depended upon to perform His word.[87]

Faith grows from abiding in the Vine[88] and having a personal relationship with Jesus. It deepens as we meditate on the word, saturate ourselves in it, and memorise it till we have a word in season for those who are weary.

How does God speak to us? God is a God of relationship, and because we are so special to Him, He wants to communicate to us – mainly through the Bible – His will and His purposes and plans for us.

> All Scripture is God-breathed and is useful for teaching, rebuking, correcting and training in righteousness, so that the man of God may be thoroughly equipped for every good work.
>
> *2 Timothy 3:16-17*

We must, however, understand that it is possible to read the whole of the Bible, have intelligent theological conversations and still not be able to hear God speak. Without the revelation of the Holy Spirit there is no way of hearing God speak as it will just amount to another good read.

---

86 See Jeremiah 29:11
87 See Jeremiah 1:12
88 "I am the true vine, and My Father is the vinedresser. Every branch in Me that does not bear fruit He takes away; and every branch that bears fruit He prunes, that it may bear more fruit. You are already clean because of the word which I have spoken to you. Abide in Me, and I in you. As the branch cannot bear fruit of itself, unless it abides in the vine, neither can you, unless you abide in Me. I am the vine, you are the branches. He who abides in Me, and I in him, bears much fruit; for without Me you can do nothing. If anyone does not abide in Me, he is cast out as a branch and is withered; and they gather them and throw them into the fire, and they are burned. If you abide in Me, and My words abide in you, you will ask what you desire, and it shall be done for you. By this My Father is glorified, that you bear much fruit; so you will be My disciples." (John 15:1-8)

When the Spirit of truth comes, he will guide you into all the truth; for he will not speak on his own, but will speak whatever he hears, and he will declare to you the things that are to come.

John 16:13

You are wrong if you think you can discover God in the Bible through your own intelligence and traditional interpretations alone. Human reasoning and tradition failed the leaders of Israel during the time of Jesus. The scribes and Pharisees had all of those *and* still they missed the Messiah in their midst. Jesus rebuked them with these words:

"You search the scriptures because you think that in them you have eternal life; and it is they that testify on my behalf. Yet you refuse to come to me to have life."

John 5:39-40

FAITH EXPANDS BY FOCUSING ON GOD'S VISION

Jesus' human vision went beyond the cross when He embraced God's larger vision to be the Saviour of mankind:

...fixing our eyes on Jesus, the pioneer and perfecter of faith. For the joy set before him he endured the cross, scorning its shame, and sat down at the right hand of the throne of God.

Hebrews 12:2 (NIV)

Ezekiel saw in a vision a valley of dry bones, which represented the house of Israel. The situation was beyond hopeless. But the Lord told him to prophesy to these bones these words:

"Dry bones, hear the word of the LORD! This is what the Sovereign LORD says to these bones: I will make breath enter you, and you will come to life."

Ezekiel 37:4

Ezekiel did as he was told and the dry bones became living men, but there was no breath in them. Then the Lord said again:

"Prophesy to the breath; prophesy, son of man, and say to it, 'This is what the Sovereign LORD says: Come, breath, from the four winds and breathe into these slain, that they may live.'" So I prophesied as he commanded me, and breath

entered them; they came to life and stood up on their feet—a
vast army.

Ezekiel 37:9-10

Ezekiel overcame because he was able to see beyond what clearly was a state of total hopelessness into a remarkable future for God's people. He left the complexities of creation to the Creator and just declared the word of the Lord.

In our lives, and indeed in the body of Christ, how do we view our situation? Are we overwhelmed with our realities? Do we meander in the darkness of denominational issues and spiritual muddiness? Or do we leave the complexities of our situation to God by surrendering our doubts to Him?

FAITH IS REINFORCED BY LARGE FOOTPRINTS

The Bible is saturated with marvellous accounts of God's interventions, such as the parting of the Red Sea and the Jordan, to constantly remind ourselves of our covenant with a great and mighty God.

When Joshua and the children of Israel had crossed over the dry path through the river Jordan, they were commanded to place twelve stones on the west bank at Gilgal. These stones would stand as landmarks and a memorial to testify of the Lord's goodness when He led them into the Promised Land.[89]

What are the landmarks in your personal walk of faith with God? Healing? Witnessing? Power prayer? Restoration of relationships? Mighty moves of the Holy Spirit? Hold on to them. Play them back in your mind every time doubt and fear creep in. Remind yourself that you are a child of the living God and that He is both faithful and responds to faith.

Hebrews 11:4-3 catalogues the deeds of the people of faith who rose up to the call of God upon their life regardless of the obvious and unbelievable challenges that confronted them. Here is the closing section:

By faith the walls of Jericho fell down after they were encircled
for seven days. By faith the harlot Rahab did not perish with

---

[89] See Joshua 4:6-7

those who did not believe, when she had received the spies with peace.

And what more shall I say? For the time would fail me to tell of Gideon and Barak and Samson and Jephthah, also of David and Samuel and the prophets: who through faith subdued kingdoms, worked righteousness, obtained promises, stopped the mouths of lions, quenched the violence of fire, escaped the edge of the sword, out of weakness were made strong, became valiant in battle, turned to flight the armies of the aliens. Women received their dead raised to life again.

Others were tortured, not accepting deliverance, that they might obtain a better resurrection. Still others had trial of mockings and scourgings, yes, and of chains and imprisonment. They were stoned, they were sawn in two, were tempted, were slain with the sword. They wandered about in sheepskins and goatskins, being destitute, afflicted, tormented—of whom the world was not worthy. They wandered in deserts and mountains, in dens and caves of the earth.

And all these, having obtained a good testimony through faith, did not receive the promise, God having provided something better for us, that they should not be made perfect apart from us.

Hebrews 11:4-30

Every time I read this account, I am so encouraged by the fact that these heroes were everyday people like you and me. They held their ground and overcame by the faith that God had planted in their hearts and by the words of their testimonies. These were far from perfect people, but like Rahab (a woman with a colourful past) and Samson and Gideon (who had many character flaws) they are honoured in God's hall of fame because they embraced God's vision and answered the call. And nothing pleases God more than faith!

As each of us runs our own race, I would urge all of us to:

- *run with perseverance*

  Therefore, since we are surrounded by such a great cloud of witnesses, let us throw off everything that hinders and the sin that so easily entangles. And let us run with perseverance the race marked out for us

Hebrews 12:1 (NIV)

- *run with purpose*

  Do you not know that in a race all the runners run, but only one gets the prize? Run in such a way as to get the prize. Everyone who competes in the games goes into strict training. They do it to get a crown that will not last, but we do it to get a crown that will last forever. Therefore I do not run like someone running aimlessly; I do not fight like a boxer beating the air. No, I strike a blow to my body and make it my slave so that after I have preached to others, I myself will not be disqualified for the prize.

  1 Corinthians 9:24-27 (NIV)

Right now, God is looking at His plan for His Church in anticipation of His great move. It will be our Day of Pentecost. Let us look with eyes of faith at where God is looking. It would have been easy for Abel, Enoch and Abraham to disbelieve God – but, *no,* they chose to trust Him. Ezekiel could simply have said to God, "You must be joking! Look, can't you see the bones are very dry and there is no hope for them?" But, *no,* he left that argument to God and prophesied.

Dear friend, be encouraged by this verse:

...being confident of this, that he who began a good work in you will carry it on to completion until the day of Christ Jesus.

Philippians 1:6 (NIV)

Let us look beyond our material reality into the invisible that can transform our fears into faith and doubts into trust in God, the Master of the universe. We are called to be different, to see differently, act differently and gain a different destination from the crowd.

CHAPTER SEVEN

Praying the Lord's Way

"Therefore I tell you, whatever you ask for in prayer, believe that you have received it, and it will be yours."

Mark 11:24

Just as faith is the catalyst for your miracle, prayer is the conduit for transporting your message to God. What is prayer? Simply put, prayer is a two-way communication between you and God as your Father. Jesus often addressed the Father using the Greek words *Pater* or *Abba* meaning 'Father', 'Papa' or 'Daddy', words that even a child would instinctively use. It means, let us get into a relationship here, not from a place of distance but from a place of covenant as a child of God. The scriptures tell us that Jesus Christ "has obtained a more excellent ministry, inasmuch as He is also Mediator of a better covenant, which was established on better promises"[90]. As a result, we have the privilege to participate in the blessings of being one of God's own, especially if we recognised Jesus' ministry of reconciliation and walk according to the grace and precepts of God. Covenant relationship with God is more than a contractual agreement between two parties; it is a divine bond that can only be broken by both parties (God and man), instead of one party as with a material contract.

So prayer, from the simple cry of "Father" or "Jesus" to a formal prayer, is reaching out to God from wherever we are. It is keeping that daily appointment with Him in the secret place and abiding under the shadow of the Almighty. It is trusting in Him as our refuge and our fortress.[91] It is coming to Him with a humble and contrite heart in all our brokenness to seek His face, casting our burden on Him knowing that He cares.[92]

---

[90] Hebrews 8:6-8
[91] See Psalm 91:1-2
[92] See Psalm 51:7; 1 Peter 5:7

The Bible tells us to "pray without ceasing"[93]. How is that possible while we are at work, doing our chores, interacting with others, watching football and even sleeping? It has to do with having an attitude of prayer and consecrating our waking and sleeping hours to God. It's making time to start the day with Him in praise and worship and making it the last thing we do before bedtime. It's sending quick love messages to Him even in our busiest moments. It's calling upon His name when we are in difficulty. It's giving Him the glory by excelling in our work. It's sharing His goodness with others. How wonderful it is to have an open conversation with the Giver of all good things!

But the basic question that is on everybody's mind is, "How do I pray effectively?"

This was the very question Jesus' disciples asked of Him, seeing that He spent so much time praying and that all His prayers were answered. Jesus gave them an illustration with the Lord's Prayer:

> *Our Father in heaven,*
> *Hallowed be Your name.*
> *Your kingdom come.*
> *Your will be done*
> *On earth as it is in heaven.*
> *Give us this day our daily bread.*
> *And forgive us our debts,*
> *As we forgive our debtors.*
> *And do not lead us into temptation,*
> *But deliver us from the evil one.*
> *For Yours is the kingdom and the power and the glory forever.*
> *Amen*
>
> *Matthew 6:9-13*

Christians around the world read the Lord's Prayer, recite it and sing it, while some churches services are never concluded without repeating it. In fact, the Lord's Prayer has become a set formula that some people *say* without giving an iota of *thought* to it – in which case it seems to me like a religious ritual.

Jesus was always into relationship and extemporaneity. The last thing He wanted was parroted or repetitive prayer, for He said:

---

[93] 1 Thessalonians 5:17

"And when you pray, do not use vain repetitions as the heathen do. For they think that they will be heard for their many words."

Matthew 6:7

The word "vain" here means 'empty' or 'useless', so Jesus is warning us that saying long repetitive prayers will not be of much use. Our Heavenly Father is not concerned with how long, how eloquent or formal our prayers are, but what He desires is "truth in the inward parts"[94].

Note also that Jesus said, "Pray *like* this," not, "Pray this prayer."[95] Viewed in this way, we should use the Lord's Prayer more as an attitude of prayer as well as a guide. I believe the Lord wants us to use this pattern of prayer as a kind of template, and to understand the spiritual principles underlying it.

What we must understand about the Lord's Prayer is that it was a pre-New-Covenant prayer, in that Jesus had yet not gone to the cross, He had not yet risen and Pentecost had not happened. But because of Calvary, our prayer is now so much more enriched because it is founded on a new boldness as sons of God, who are now led by the Holy Spirit.[96]

Likewise the Spirit also helps in our weaknesses. For we do not know what we should pray for as we ought, but the Spirit Himself makes intercession for us...

Romans 8:26

The Lord's Prayer

Let us look at the elements of the Lord's Prayer and see how we can capture the spirit of it in our own prayer. It starts with:

Our Father in heaven,
Hallowed be Your name

What a wonderful way to open our prayer! We approach the Father by acknowledging that He is omnipotent, omniscient and omnipresent. He is the Sovereign Ruler of all and in Him all things hold together. Jesus Christ, who is the express image of the invincible God, taught us to start

---

94 Psalm 51:6
95 See Matthew 6:9
96 See Hebrews 4:16; Romans 8:14

by calling on the Father who must be hallowed, honoured, revered and adored.

When we hallow His name, we are coming into His presence as one would approach a king with gifts. What are our gifts? Our praise and thanksgiving. Remember that God is enthroned in the praises of His people.[97] Come into His presence with praise and singing:

Make a joyful shout to the LORD, all you lands!

> *Serve the LORD with gladness;*
> *Come before His presence with singing.*
> *Know that the LORD, He is God...*

Psalm 100:1-3

We also enter into His presence in the spirit of thanksgiving regardless of what we are going through. We are called to give thanks in whatever circumstances as this is the gateway to faith-filled and joyful expectation that God will surely speak to us.

> *Your kingdom come.*
> *Your will be done*
> *On earth as it is in heaven.*

We are to invite and call down the actual kingdom of God here on earth where the will of God prevails over every other, for He is the King of kings and Lord of lords. So we acknowledge God's supremacy over our lives by allowing His will to be done in our lives and in the lives of those we love.

What is the order of the things we pray for? Our natural tendency would be to pray for ourselves first and then our family, our community, our nation and the nations to which we are called to pray. But this is not the biblical order of prayer:

> *Therefore I exhort first of all that supplications, prayers, intercessions, and giving of thanks be made for all men, for kings and all who are in authority, that we may lead a quiet and peaceable life in all godliness and reverence.*

1 Timothy 2:1-2 (emphasis added)

---

[97] See Psalm 22:3

The direction of God's prayer is outward and then inward. The first priority is for "kings and all who are in authority"; that means the government of the day. Why is this so? That we may lead a quiet and peaceable life in all godliness and reverence. Whether we like the government or not, it is the governing authority appointed by God and we are to respect it as unto God.[98] This does not mean that we cannot criticise the government for its failings but we should do so constructively for the purpose of improvement. Most governments are under tremendous pressure because of global turbulence, from economic struggles to terrorism and, as believers, our prayers should be directed at uplifting our leaders so that they govern wisely, justly and ethically.

Stand in the gap for your nation and its leaders by repenting on their behalf for national sins.

> *...if My people who are called by My name will humble themselves, and pray and seek My face, and turn from their wicked ways, then I will hear from heaven, and will forgive their sin and heal their land.*
>
> 2 Chronicles 7:14

As I pray for my nation, especially the prime minister and parliament, I pray for their good health, safety and protection against all the devices of the evil one, including witchcraft attacks. I pray the Lord's destiny for this nation, that we will have the freedom to preach the gospel so that revival will spring up and light will flood every dark place. I pray for the church to arise and exercise her position as the light and the salt and lead others to Jesus. I declare that the righteousness of Christ will exalt this nation.[99]

After you pray for your nation, pray for Israel as we are commended to do. Pray especially that spiritual blindness will be removed and they will recognise their Messiah. Declare that all Israel will be saved.[100] Pray for the peace of Jerusalem and great blessing on those nations who have prophetically 'established Jerusalem' as the nation's capital by setting up their embassies there.[101]

---

98 See Romans 13:1-2
99 See Proverbs 14:34
100 See Romans 11:26
101 See Isaiah 62:6-7

Then pray for the nations that God has led you to pray for, declaring a mighty move of God sweeping across them. Declare that the Babylon system (i.e. immorality, corruption and false religion) is fallen.[102] Proclaim that, "The kingdoms of this world are become the kingdoms of our Lord, and of his Christ; and he shall reign for ever and ever."[103]

After this, pray for all your personal, family and community needs. Declare salvation and deliverance over members who are still lost; speak unity into division; thank the Lord for giving your children a teachable spirit: "All my children shall be taught of the Lord and great shall be the peace of my family. In righteousness they shall be established!"[104]

We can also pray the Scriptures over our lives. For example, Psalm 107 connects our hopes with the aspirations of God's people in the Old Testament. Sin and disobedience had brought the people into bondage but when they repented and cried out to God, He rescued them every time.

Here's how you can personalise it for yourself:

> LORD, I give thanks to You, for You are good!
> For Your mercy endures forever.
> Let the redeemed of the LORD say so,
> Because You have redeemed me from the hand of the enemy...
> I wandered about in distress
>   because I had strayed away from You;
> I was lost with no protection.
> Hungry and thirsty,
> And emotionally distraught.
> Then I cried out to You in my trouble,
> And You delivered me out of my distress.
>
> *Based on Psalm 107:1-2,4-6*

GIVE US THIS DAY OUR DAILY BREAD

Many pious people interpret this request as saying that God will supply just enough for our basic needs – not more, because He is against riches.

---

[102] See Revelation 14:8
[103] Revelation 11:15 (KJV)
[104] See Isaiah 54:13-14

But this is against the whole thrust of the Scriptures which speak of God's provision for His people. After all, we are inheritors of God's blessing upon Abraham.[105] God's desire is that we prosper and are in health even as our soul prospers.[106] And God shall supply all of our needs according to His riches in glory by Christ Jesus.[107] He came to give us life and give it more abundantly.[108] And He takes pleasure in the prosperity (*shalom*) of His servant[109], because when we prosper, He is glorified.

Our prosperity is determined both by God's generosity and by the law of sowing and reaping:

> *He who sows sparingly will also reap sparingly, and he who sows bountifully will also reap bountifully. So let each one give as he purposes in his heart, not grudgingly or of necessity; for God loves a cheerful giver. And God is able to make all grace abound toward you, that you, always having all sufficiency in all things, may have an abundance for every good work.*
>
> 2 Corinthians 9:6-8

I'm sure it's safe to say that of all the prayers that people pray, it the one about finances that is the most frequent. That is a pressing need, especially when the expenses keep mounting. But God wants to reassure us that He will provide and wants us to stop worrying.

> *"Therefore do not worry, saying, 'What shall we eat?' or 'What shall we drink?' or 'What shall we wear?'... For your heavenly Father knows that you need all these things. But seek first the kingdom of God and His righteousness, and all these things shall be added to you. Therefore do not worry about tomorrow, for tomorrow will worry about its own things."*
>
> Matthew 6:31-34

Tell Him that you are trusting in Him with all your heart and not leaning on your own understanding; in all your ways you are submitting to Him, and He is making every crooked path straight.[110] Declare that

---

[105] See Genesis 12:3
[106] See 2 John 3
[107] See Philippians 4:19
[108] See John 10:10
[109] See Psalm 35:27
[110] See Proverbs 3:5-6

promotion and power come from nowhere on earth, but only from God. He promotes one and deposes another.[111]

> *And forgive us our debts,*
> *As we forgive our debtors.*

In the same teaching on prayer, Jesus emphasized the paramount importance of forgiveness:

> *"For if you forgive men their trespasses, your heavenly Father will also forgive you. But if you do not forgive men their trespasses, neither will your Father forgive your trespasses."*
>
> *Matthew 6:14-15*

This aspect of the Lord's prayer seems to be the toughest for many people, who like to rehearse the wrong done to them and hold on to their right to be offended. But this is totally at variance with the heart of God, who made a way of forgiveness through His Son.

Jesus consistently forgave throughout His ministry, from releasing forgiveness on the woman caught in adultery, to "Father, forgive them" at the cross.[112] To have the same spirit with Christ, I want to plead with you to revisit Calvary so that you can receive strength to forgive others and be yourself forgiven. Living a life of unforgiveness will hurt you and destroy you eternally.

What is forgiveness? Forgiveness is the act of releasing an offender from the offence committed so that they can go free. Literally, forgiveness means 'to let go', 'to stop blaming or being angry with someone for something that person has done, to stop punishing them for some wrong'.

Forgiveness does not mean disregarding the offence, living in denial or letting others take advantage of you. Rather, it simply means to release the person of the guilt.

God has provided forgiveness for us through Christ's sacrifice.[113]

> *If we confess our sins, He is faithful and just to forgive us our sins and to cleanse us from all unrighteousness.*
>
> *1 John 1:9*

---

[111] See Psalm 75:6-7
[112] See John 8:1-11; Luke 23:34
[113] See Romans 5:8

All we have to do is come to God and say we are sorry, and it's done. We must remember, however, that God does not forgive people who are guilty of wilful, malicious sin, who refuse to acknowledge their wrongdoing or forgive others.

This might be a fitting time to go over Jesus' parable of the unforgiving servant.[114] The story is set in three scenes. Scene One takes place inside the throne room of a king, Scene Two is outside in a palace corridor, Scene Three is back in the throne room. The story tells of two worlds: the dog-eat-dog world as we know it and the world of compassion that God inhabits.

Scene One: The king discovers that his servant owes him an enormous amount of money and threatens to throw him in prison till he repays his debt. The servant falls to his knees, crying out for mercy. Against all reason, the king goes out of his way and forgives the servant, cancelling his huge debt.

At the throne room of God, mercy and goodness flow to us beyond imagination. If the cross of Christ delivers one message, it is unmerited freedom and forgiveness. Christ gave His own life to earn the forgiveness for our sins, something we cannot achieve through our own righteousness.

Scene Two: The forgiven debtor now encounters a fellow servant in the corridor who owes him a small amount. He seizes him by the collar and tries to strangle him to squeeze out some payments. You would imagine that the fair thing to do would be to be gracious to his debtor and forgive, remembering the huge burden that was lifted off him. One would think that mercy received would result in mercy given. However, he refuses to show mercy; instead, he is ready to boot him to the nearest prison indefinitely. Alas, the palace corridor as we know it today remains stuck with forgiven unforgivers.

For many, forgiveness is difficult. We conveniently forget – or maybe we've never acknowledged – that we are forgiven sinners, debtors let off the hook. Or we pay lip service to it, but our heart nurses the offence. My brother, my sister, forgiveness is not an option; it is an imperative. It is difficult, it is costly. But know that when we forgive, we die to the world as we know it in order to usher in the kingdom of God.

---

[114] See Matthew 18:23-35

Scene Three: But look what happens when the king finds out. He summons the servant and says:

> "*'You wicked servant. I forgave you all that debt, because you begged me. Should you not also have had mercy on your fellow servant, even as I had mercy on you?' His lord was angry, and delivered him to the tormentors, until he should pay all that was due. So my heavenly Father will also do to you, if you do not each forgive your brother from your heart."*
>
> *Matthew 18:32-34 (NHEB)*

The story ends with a serious warning. If we abuse God's immeasurable forgiveness and choose to remain in unforgiveness, we subject ourselves to the tormentors. Who are these tormentors? It's a state of mental unrest marked by any number of psychosomatic ailments. It's a life of bondage because we chose to be held captive by our revenge and self-righteousness, rather than live the life and peace and contentment that forgiveness from the cross offers.

> *And do not lead us into temptation,*
> *But deliver us from the evil one.*

One of the greatest deceptions of our modern secular age is that the devil is a figment of our imagination and that anyone who mentions the devil is just being superstitious. As a result, many Christians have their guard down and are complacent. But listen to Peter's warning:

> *Be on your guard and stay awake. Your enemy, the devil, is like a roaring lion, sneaking around to find someone to attack.*
>
> *1 Peter 5:8 (CEV)*

The devil has one mission, and that is to steal, to kill and to destroy.[115] Who? You!

Another misconception is that God is the one who tempts us into sin. But this notion is refuted by James who tells us it is we who are enticed by our own lusts.[116] Remember the foolish young man enticed by the harlot in Proverbs?

---

[115] See John 10:10
[116] See James 1:14

A young man devoid of understanding,
Passing along the street near her corner;
And he took the path to her house...
And there a woman met him,
With the attire of a harlot, and a crafty heart...

Proverbs 7:7,8,10

Do you see that his heart was seeking adventure because he chose to take the path to her house? No, the Lord will never tempt but He has promised to protect His children in the hour of temptation. He will even provide a way of escape, so that we may be able to endure it.[117]

For Yours is the kingdom and the power and the glory forever.
Amen

Having committed everything to God we must now rest in the assurance that God is absolutely in charge. He is Sovereign and all power belongs to Him from eternity to eternity.

"I am God, and there is no other; I am God, and there is none like me, declaring the end from the beginning and from ancient times things not yet done, saying, 'My counsel shall stand, and I will accomplish all my purpose.'"

Isaiah 46:9-10 (NIV)

Let me conclude by encouraging you never to allow your prayer life to become a monotonous religious ritual. The pattern of the Lord's Prayer should rather encourage us that we have a unique relationship with God. Even when answers are slow to come, let us keep asking, keep seeking and keep knocking till we see our breakthrough.

---

[117] See 1 Corinthians 10:13

CHAPTER EIGHT

Detoxing Our Soul

Contrast toxic religion with the pure gospel.
Religion is all about what I do.
The gospel is all about what Jesus has done.

Craig Groeschel; Soul Detox

My heart is heavy as I begin this chapter, heavy because of the spiritual condition of the church of Jesus Christ. Like a fish trying to breathe in a pond that has been contaminated with toxic waste, I am grieved by the spiritual atmosphere over the Body worldwide, especially in Britain and the West. Has our condition of apathy, lawlessness and spiritual contamination affected you too? Are you grieved, too?

In this chapter we need to address the serious issue of contamination in our lives. We need to understand what has caused such toxicity and what the remedies are. The Merriam-Webster dictionary defines toxicity as "containing or being poisonous material especially when capable of causing death or serious debilitation". It follows that detoxing is the process of halting or expelling the toxic substances from the body. The idea behind it is that there is a need for periodical cleansing of the 'toxic waste' from our body system in order to stay healthy.

As we broach the subject of toxicity within the Body of Christ, I am reminded of that scene when Jesus confronts the traders in the temple.

Cleansing the Temple

Now, the Passover of the Jews was at hand, and Jesus went up to Jerusalem. And He found in the temple those who sold oxen and sheep and doves, and the money-changers doing business. When He had made a whip of cords, He drove them all out of the temple, with the sheep and the oxen, and poured out the changers' money and overturned the tables. And He said to those who sold doves, "Take these things away! Do not make My Father's house a house of merchandise!" Then His disciples remembered that it was written, "Zeal for Your house has eaten Me up."[118]

The traders in the temple court were going about their usual business, so what in fact had they done wrong? What had caused Jesus such anger? Covetousness and corruption. It was true that animal sacrifice was carried out in the temple court and it was therefore necessary for many worshipers to buy the animals for the sacrifice at the temple as well as change money, if needed. The problem was that the system had become highly corrupt. The traders often took advantage of the demand during festive seasons to charge exorbitant prices, sell defective animals and short-change the currency. There was a strong suspicion that the temple authorities were complicit in all these dealings because they controlled all the trading activities in the temple. Add to this the hypocrisy and self-interest of the Jewish leaders, many of whom Jesus Himself rebuked as "whitewashed tombs"[119] and you have a picture of the corrupt system.

How ironic that all these practices were going on in a place designated for prayer to a holy God!

To bring home the severity of the wrongdoing, I want to take you to Leviticus 14:33-42. This passage talks about the ritualistic cleansing of houses that had become contaminated. Most translations refer to this contamination as "leprosy"; others as contamination by mildew. It was serious enough for the owner to contact the priest who would go through various procedures to remove the mildew from the walls. If he found that the mildew had gone deeper than the wall surface and later had spread, he would order that the stones be removed and dumped outside the town. Meanwhile, the walls had to be thoroughly scraped and new stones replace the contaminated ones. If, after a final inspection, the priest found that the contamination had spread beyond control, he would declare the whole house defiled. Here then is what happens:

> *It must be torn down, and all its stones, timbers, and plaster must be carried out of town to the place designated as ceremonially unclean. Those who enter the house during the period of quarantine will be ceremonially unclean until evening...*
>
> Leviticus 14:45-46 (emphasis added)

---

[118] See John 2:13-17
[119] Matthew 23:27

Dear reader, do you at once catch the revelation and see the parallel between the defiled house and the church? Let us examine all the elements together. Who is the owner of the house? It is God Himself who is the head of His holy temple. Who is the ultimate priest? Jesus is the high priest, who is responsible for keeping the house of His Father – the church – clean and undefiled. During His time on earth Jesus was already exercising His high priestly function by inspecting the temple to see that it was properly maintained. Imagine His outrage when He sees such desecration in that place!

In the process of writing this section I feel strongly impressed upon by the Lord to pay attention to Psalm 69 verse 9:

"...zeal for Your house has eaten me up."

This is the exact same line as John 2:17. I began to sense the intense shame and emotional pain the Lord suffered when He was rejected by His own people for His zeal for His house.

Because for Your sake I have borne reproach;
Shame has covered my face.
I have become a stranger to my brothers,
And an alien to my mother's children;
Because zeal for Your house has eaten me up,
And the reproaches of those who reproach You have fallen on
me.

Psalm 59:7-9

If you experience isolation, rejection, humiliation because of your own outrage at the things happening around you, this is the psalm to return to. It's a blend of David's emotions and the Lord's emotions on the cross, and it vividly expresses the isolation associated with righteous indignation.

Do you see the parallel between the house stones that were cast out and Jesus who is the stone the builders rejected which has become the chief cornerstone?[120] The very stone that was cast out of the city gates became the stone that made the building whole.

In the temple grounds, Jesus was then quizzed by the Jews:

"What sign do You show to us, since You do these things?"

---

[120] See Matthew 21:42

Jesus answered and said to them, "Destroy this temple, and in three days I will raise it up."

Then the Jews said, "It has taken forty-six years to build this temple, and will You raise it up in three days?"

But He was speaking of the temple of His body. Therefore, when He had risen from the dead, His disciples remembered that He had said this to them; and they believed the Scripture and the word which Jesus had said.

John 2:18-22

In answer to the Jews, the sign that Jesus pointed to was His own death and resurrection. By this, we know that the temple in Jerusalem symbolised His own body and, by extension, His wider Body, the church. We, too, are the temple of the Holy Spirit, who resides in us, and we represent Jesus on earth.

Given the backdrop of the Leviticus 14 commandment, our role as the temple comes into focus when Jesus cleanses the temple a second time at His final Passover. This episode is recorded in the other three synoptic Gospels.[121]

And he entered the temple and began to drive out those who sold and those who bought in the temple, and he overturned the tables of the money-changers and the seats of those who sold pigeons. And he would not allow anyone to carry anything through the temple. And he was teaching them and saying to them, "Is it not written, 'My house shall be called a house of prayer for all the nations'? But you have made it a den of robbers."

Mark 11:15-17

Same scene as the first Passover. Nothing had changed. All Jesus' warnings from the earlier inspection had fallen on deaf ears. Instead of making that house a house of prayer, the leaders continued their plunder, acting no differently from the Canaanite traders in the surrounding land.

The defilement of the house had spread to not only the house but also its occupants because the leaven of sin contaminates everything. According to the law, there remains only one remedy: *destroy the house.*

---

[121] See Matthew 21:12-13; Mark 11:12-17; Luke 19:45-46

Jesus had already prophesied the destruction of the physical temple when He looked out on to the city and wept:

> *"If you had known, even you, especially in this your day, the things that make for your peace! But now they are hidden from your eyes. For days will come upon you when your enemies will build an embankment around you, surround you and close you in on every side, and level you, and your children within you, to the ground; and they will not leave in you one stone upon another, because you did not know the time of your visitation."*
>
> *Luke 19:42-44*

History tells us that the temple and the holy city were completely destroyed by the Roman armies in A.D. 70 – not a stone was left standing. Since that day the temple has never been rebuilt.

The New Temple of God

That's not the end of the story; it's only the beginning. By Jesus' death and resurrection, He has rescued the house and set up His temple in our hearts. We are that temple of God built from new and living stones, cleansed by the blood of Jesus:

> *And coming to Him as to a living stone which has been rejected by men, but is choice and precious in the sight of God, you also, as living stones, are being built up as a spiritual house for a holy priesthood, to offer up spiritual sacrifices acceptable to God through Jesus Christ.*
>
> *1 Peter 2:4-5 (NASB)*

And we are more than living stones:

> *... but you are <u>a chosen race, a royal priesthood, a holy nation, a people for God's own possession,</u> so that you may proclaim the excellencies of him who has called you out of darkness into his marvelous light.*
>
> *1 Peter 2:9 (NASB, emphasis added)*

Jesus is the High Priest in heaven making intercession for us. But He has made us His chosen generation, His holy people and His royal priests. We now have that awesome responsibility of making this temple of our own hearts, and that of the church and our nation, holy, separated unto

114

Him, that we may show forth His marvellous light through the approaching darkness that will cover the whole earth.

Jesus' second cleansing of the temple was His final inspection of the house of Jerusalem – and it was found to be beyond repair. This defilement of the temple was symbolic of the fundamental failure of Israel as a nation, for instead of witnessing to the nations, Israel was steeped in sin.

Jesus' final cleansing of the house of God will be His end-time cleansing of the church and the nations. He has already warned us of the state of apostasy and depravity of man when He comes back:

> *"But as the days of Noah were, so also will the coming of the Son of Man be. For as in the days before the flood, they were eating and drinking, marrying and giving in marriage, until the day that Noah entered the ark, and did not know until the flood came and took them all away, so also will the coming of the Son of Man be."*

Matthew 24:37-39

Why is the mention of the days of Noah so significant? Because the wickedness on the earth had reached its fullness with every imaginable perversion so that God had to destroy it in the flood. Only the life of one righteous man and his family were spared because he believed in God and made the ark. That ark for us is represented by the ark of covenant, Jesus Christ, who has covenanted with us and given us the Holy Spirit as a seal.

Writing to the Thessalonians Paul reminded them of the day of the Lord which will come like a thief in the night. There are clear choices we can make:

- *either* we try to understand the nature and the call of God and realign ourselves with it;
- *or* we ignore all the signs and live recklessly as if there were no tomorrow, and bury the gifts we are endowed with in the sand.

Contamination in Our Society

What has caused such contamination in our modern society? I believe it's our personal sin, which, when full-blown, gives rise to corporate sin that defiles the whole Body:

A little leaven leavens the whole lump.

Galatians 5:9

PERSONAL SIN

We may argue that our sin is personal and that it's nobody's business. But look at it this way. A woman may decide to have an abortion because she feels she has a right to her own body. But when society just looks on and does not take responsibility for it, it's the same as condoning the murder of an innocent baby. Consequently, the ground cries out to God for blood and the community is defiled.[122]

Sometimes, for the sake of political correctness, society says and does nothing when public sin takes place. Take, for example, David's sin with Bathsheba, not just the adultery but the cover-up which involved the murder of Bathsheba's husband. David went on sinning for a whole year and on the surface it looked as if no one was offended. After all, he was king! It took the courage of Nathan the prophet to confront David (indirectly through a story) so that his eyes were open to the enormity of his crime against God, and David repented with great remorse.[123] Out of this repentance came this most beautiful cry for forgiveness from a broken and contrite man who wanted nothing but honesty in his inward parts between him and his God:

> *Create in me a clean heart, O God,*
> *And renew a steadfast spirit within me.*
> *Do not cast me away from Your presence,*
> *And do not take Your Holy Spirit from me.*
> *Restore to me the joy of Your salvation,*
> *And uphold me by Your generous Spirit.*
> *Then I will teach transgressors Your ways,*
> *And sinners shall be converted to You.*
> *Deliver me from the guilt of bloodshed, O God,*
> *The God of my salvation...*

Psalm 51:10-14

What is sin (Greek: *hamartia*) but 'missing the mark'? It's not the big sins but the small incremental acts of missing the mark that start to harden the heart and breed deception and spiritual blindness. The church

---

[122] See Genesis 4:10
[123] See 2 Samuel 12:1-13

at Laodicea were blinded by their worldly success into thinking they were doing well. But this is what Jesus had to say:

> *"I know your works, that you are neither cold nor hot. I could wish you were cold or hot. So then, because you are lukewarm, and neither cold nor hot, I will vomit you out of My mouth. Because you say, 'I am rich, have become wealthy, and have need of nothing'—and do not know that you are wretched, miserable, poor, blind, and naked..."*
>
> *Revelation 3:15-17*

Let us examine our own hearts and see where we have missed the mark. The more obvious ones would be ungodly soul ties,[124] sins of the flesh, negative thoughts and confessions. But the more devious ones could be found in our preoccupation with self and in our hidden agendas – perhaps in seeking the anointing more than The Anointed One.

Right now, let us recognise the depth of our sin and how it has hurt our relationship with God, and let us cry out to Him in our brokenness. He will surely revive us as He revived David with the joy of his salvation.

THE CHURCH

When I comment on the spiritual condition of the church, I am looking at the entire body of believers. It is we who are responsible for the spiritual condition of the church and moral decay of our society as a consequence of our apathy. I am not targeting any particular denomination or leadership hierarchy, but I am addressing all of God's people who can discern the times. I am confining my remarks to the Western church though, because this is where postmodernism (and now post-truth) has made its greatest impact.

Like Israel, the church is expected to be the light and salt of its culture in terms of upholding God's standards and advancing God's kingdom. Yet even as Israel did not hold firm to its distinctiveness but indulged in the perversions of the surrounding nations, so also has the Western church largely failed to uphold its moral standards but has absorbed the trajectory of a drifting society. I say drifting because, by and large, revered traditional values such as the sanctity of marriage, the family, the

---

[124] Ungodly soul ties: things that captivate and enslave your mind to the extent that you no longer are able to respect your body anymore; see 1 Corinthians 6:18-19

117

upbringing of the young and the right of the unborn to life have been severely eroded – and now we hear liberal left voices even raising questions about gender binarism!

Some of the values the church has absorbed are not unlike those of the merchants in the temple court. Let's get into specifics.

MARKETPLACE MENTALITY

I call this the 'merchandising' of faith all for the sake of 'propagating the gospel'. We now see mega churches with a preoccupation for producing videos, books and other marketing material – ostensibly to reach out. But could money be the main driver? We offer a pop culture to reach out to millennials. But are we trading holiness for hype?

It's true there are vibrant mega churches all over the world that raise up fiery evangelists, prayer warriors and intercessors. I am referring more to mega and aspiring mega churches that in their quest for numbers preach a watered-down message. The only way to attract the crowds is to adopt a seeker-friendly posture, with no cutting edge. "God is a God of love and will accept you as you are," they say but there is no emphasis on holiness and the transformative power of the word. And so, we accommodate all manner of social vices and people with no respect for godliness and standards. We simply forget that we are instructed in Romans:

> *Do not conform to the pattern of this world but be transformed by the renewing of your mind. Then you will be able to test and approve what God's will is—his good, pleasing and perfect will.*
>
> *Romans 12:2 (NIV)*

Yet people are made comfortable and this is called a 'welcoming church'. In order to please, scriptures are conveniently left out, re-interpreted or redefined to suit. We preach on love but not commitment, with no boundaries between what is acceptable behaviour and what is sin.

The seeker-friendly church preaches anything that is palatable to the ear, the church is then turned into an entertainment circus and those who lead argue that unless we have these attractions, the people will not come to church. The reason people do not come to church may be because these places have become *ichabod*[125] churches where the glory of God has long left the building. Experience has taught me that the Word of God that once was the centre character of the church has little or no place in some churches anymore. For example, for a wedding the pastor is told, "Do not preach because it is the couple's happy day," and for a funeral the pastor is told, "Do not preach. The family are grieving." At Christmas time, they say, "Do not preach. It is a family occasion," and on Sunday morning they say to you, "Do not exceed fifteen minutes because people have a very short attention span." On and on the excuses go. Passionate preaching no longer has a place in some churches anymore.

You might have experienced real change in your life at the beginning of your walk with God and this change is meant to be sustained; it is beyond a simple emotive experience of enthusiasm that easily wane, it is an experience of *metanoia*.

> But God will not be mocked. As He chastised Israel, so will He chastise His people, for judgment will start in the house of God: "For the time is come that judgment must begin at the house of God: and if it first begin at us, what shall the end be of them that obey not the gospel of God?"
>
> 1 Peter 4:17 (KJV)

This is God's response to all our vain attempts at doing religion:

> Whom do you mock,
> making faces and sticking out your tongues?
> You children of sinners and liars!
> You worship your idols with great passion
> beneath the oaks and under every green tree.
> You sacrifice your children down in the valleys,
> among the jagged rocks in the cliffs.
> You have committed adultery on every high mountain.
> There you have worshiped idols
> and have been unfaithful to me.
> You have gone to Molech [read child sacrifice, read abortions]
> with olive oil and many perfumes,

---

125 *Ichabod* (Hebrew word): "The glory is departed from Israel"; see 1 Samuel 4:19-22

> *Let's see if your idols can save you*
> *when you cry to them for help.*
> *Why, a puff of wind can knock them down!*
> *If you just breathe on them, they fall over!*
>
> *Isaiah 57:4-12*

THE REMEDY: *METANOIA*

Read Luke 13:1-9. As apostate and corrupt as we have become, God is calling us back to Him again. His hands extend forgiveness if we would come to Him weeping for our sins and the sins of the church and nation, and experience *metanoia*. *Metanoia* is a transliteration of an Ancient Greek word which means a 'change in one's way of life resulting from penitence or spiritual conversion'. You might have experienced *metanoia* yourself at some point in your life.

Why I am I using this word instead of simple 'repentance'? There are two reasons:

- To engrave the word in your hearts because the act of repentance is key to the sustenance of our Christian faith. *Metanoia* is much more than just sorrow or grief or simply a change of mind; it is the outcome of sincere regret of what had taken place occasioning from our experience of awe-inspiring spiritual conversion.
- The word 'repentance' is grossly misrepresented. Each time the word is used, most people understand it as condemnation or simply a religious mind-control tool to keep people of faith in check.

Repentance in itself is not a dirty word. It's a positive alteration of the trajectory of one's life that is consistent with the divine guidance of Scripture. Jesus said:

> *"If you love me, keep my commands."*
>
> *John 14:15*

To be able to keep God's commands there has to be *metanoia* (repentance) and this comes with responsibility: the action on our part to remain steadfast in our confession of faith in Jesus Christ. To tell people to take action or perish is in itself not a threatening instruction, but it is the reality that people have to face. Either we make a U-turn from what the Bible says is wrong or we spiral to spiritual death. The Scripture says:

> *Since, then, we know what it is to fear the Lord, we try to persuade others. What we are is plain to God, and I hope it is also plain to your conscience.*
>
> *2 Corinthians 5:11*

There is no denying that the phrase "Repent or perish!" sounds like fire and brimstone preaching sure to send shivers down our spines, maybe because of what we know or think of some die-hard Charismatic Bible-bashing Christians. But did Jesus use such phrases to keep people in line? Definitely not. The Jesus I have come to believe in is the Jesus that loves the world enough to lay down His life for all; and to everyone who accepts His offer of salvation, He gave the power to become sons and daughters of God.

God calls us to repentance through His grace, generosity, dependable love and His persistent desire to see us live a fulfilled life. This can only happen when we repent and continue to act responsibly regarding our faith in Him, as we flee from all appearances of evil prevalent in our world today. *Metanoia* liberates us and ushers us into a new and awesome life in Christ Jesus. If we humble ourselves and come back to Him like a child, He will be merciful and receive us to Himself again. Please join me as we take a closer look at the process of restoring and rebuilding our broken lives in the next chapter.

CHAPTER NINE

Arise and Build!

"For the joy of the LORD is your strength."

Nehemiah 8:10

Our journey has led us to the sad conclusion that, in spite of God's abundant grace, our postmodern society has become apostate and morally decadent. We have lost the foundations of our faith. We have lost our first love. To rebuild these foundations, we looked at the key pillars of our faith. All these rest on the assumption of a living relationship between us and our God. We must seek to restore the vital connection that has been damaged or severed. This is why we need to understand covenant.

What Is Covenant?

A covenant is a solemn and mutually binding commitment between two parties. It's the promise that God makes with us that He will restore fellowship when we repent of our sins and turn to Him through Jesus Christ. While it is a personal commitment, it is also important we see the larger picture, that it is not just about me and God but also about my brothers and sisters – the church – for God desires to build a people for Himself.

At the Last Supper, Jesus instituted the new covenant when He broke bread...

> *...and gave it to His disciples to eat, saying, "Take eat; this is My body." Then He took the wine and gave it to them saying "Drink from it, all of you. For this is My blood of the new covenant, which is shed for many for the remission of sins."*
>
> *Matthew 26:26-28*

This new covenant had already been foretold hundreds of years ago by the prophet Jeremiah:

Behold, the days are coming, says the LORD, when I will make a new covenant with the house of Israel and with the house of Judah—not according to the covenant that I made with their fathers in the day that I took them by the hand to lead them out of the land of Egypt, My covenant which they broke, though I was a husband to them, says the LORD. But this is the covenant that I will make with the house of Israel after those days, says the LORD: I will put My law in their minds, and write it on their hearts; and I will be their God, and they shall be My people.

Jeremiah 31:31-33

Interestingly, this new covenant as described in Jeremiah was made between God and "the house of Israel and ... the house of Judah". In the Matthew account, the new covenant is not exclusively with the Jews but is open to "many". That "many" incorporates all people, Jews and Gentiles alike, who come to Jesus. Why the difference? The reason is that Jeremiah was looking to a time in the distant future when all Jews would come to saving grace by the blood of Jesus and all Israel would be saved.[126] We are entering into that final lap of history in the days we live in.

All covenants in the past were shadows or imperfect blueprints of the new and final covenant between God and man. So it would be fitting to compare this new covenant with the old covenant when God's Ten Commandments were given to Moses on Mount Sinai.[127] The Ten Commandments were written on tablets of stone, whereas the laws of the new covenant are enshrined within us because of the indwelling Holy Spirit. It's the same Ten Commandments but entered into in the spirit of Christ.[128]

No longer are the laws an imposition, but they are a liberating force because they free us from the shackles of sin. Not only that, but we live by a higher principle, according to the ways preached by Jesus at the Sermon on the Mount in Matthew 5. For example, not only do we refrain from taking revenge on those who have hurt us, we also forgive them and, by God's grace, love them.

---

[126] See Romans 11:26
[127] See Exodus 12
[128] See Galatians 6:2

"Therefore you shall be perfect, just as your Father in heaven is perfect."

Matthew 5:48

What are the distinguishing marks of the new covenant? For the Jews, the old covenant through Moses was ratified with the blood of animals. In the new covenant it's the blood of Jesus:

...when Christ appeared as a high priest of the good things to come, He entered through the greater and more perfect tabernacle ... not through the blood of goats and calves, but through His own blood, He entered the holy place once for all, having obtained eternal redemption. For if the blood of goats and bulls and the ashes of a heifer sprinkling those who have been defiled sanctify for the cleansing of the flesh, how much more will the blood of Christ, who through the eternal Spirit offered Himself without blemish to God, cleanse your conscience from dead works to serve the living God?

Hebrews 9:11-15 (NASB, emphasis added)

We see here that the blood of animals could only earn temporary forgiveness of sin for the Jews. But when Jesus the perfect sacrifice shed His blood, it was once for all mankind, for all generations.

The new covenant is also the culmination of the original covenant between God and Abraham when He made him father of all nations:

"As for Me, behold, My covenant is with you, and you shall be a father of many nations ... I will make you exceedingly fruitful; and I will make nations of you, and kings shall come from you. And I will establish My covenant between Me and you and your descendants after you in their generations, for an everlasting covenant, to be God to you and your descendants after you..."

Genesis 17:4,6-7

Abraham was a Gentile too at that time and so the blessing of fruitfulness extends to all who would come into this eternal covenant as sons of Abraham, through faith in Jesus.

The mark of the covenant with Abraham was the circumcision of all male children.[129] This cutting off of the flesh was a sign of separation from sin. In the new covenant we are not circumcised in the flesh through a physical procedure. Rather, it is a circumcision of our hearts, that is, the cutting away of the sinful nature.[130]

And so, as born-again believers we have entered into the new covenant with God because of the sacrifice of Jesus, when we repent of our sins and surrender our lives to Him. It is an everlasting covenant between us and a God who is ever faithful, who will never leave us nor forsake us. Its external sign is the wine we drink at Holy Communion, which symbolises the blood of Jesus. Physical circumcision has been replaced by spiritual circumcision because we are no longer slaves to sin.

Finally, what are our obligations as new covenant believers? The answer is the same as it was for the Jews and God's people for all times:

> *You shall love the LORD your God with all your heart, with all your soul, and with all your strength.*
>
> Deuteronomy 6:5 (emphasis added)

> *You shall love your neighbor as yourself.*
>
> Leviticus 19:18 (emphasis added)

This sums up our relationship with God and with our fellowman and naturally upholds the spirit of the Ten Commandments. One application of this command is to preach the gospel to all nations.[131]

What is God's promise to all those who keep covenant? A living relationship with the Lord and a life of shalom – righteousness, peace and joy in the Holy Spirit.[132]

Rebuilding the Wall

As we look into ways of restoring our covenant with God, let's examine the Book of Nehemiah. This is a profound story of the rebuilding of the walls and gates of Jerusalem, and covenant is repeatedly invoked. What insights can we learn from Nehemiah's experience in terms of rebuilding our broken foundations?

---

[129] See Genesis 17:10-11
[130] See Colossians 2:11
[131] Matthew 28:19-20
[132] See Romans 14:17

Let me quickly take you back to the time period of Nehemiah. One hundred and forty years had lapsed since the Babylonian king Nebuchadnezzar conquered Judah, destroying its cities and sending many of the Jews into exile in Babylon. After the new power Persia conquered the Babylonians (530 BC), the Jews were allowed to return to their homeland. The Book of Nehemiah focuses on the time when a remnant of the Jews has returned from captivity in Babylon (c. 445 BC). The land was desolate, and the cities were in disarray, in the hands of foreigners and open to attack. Though they had rebuilt the temple, the walls and gates of Jerusalem were still in ruin.

What are walls and gates but our primary protection against our enemies? Spiritually, too, walls and gates speak of God's protection from demonic attack when we make Him our refuge and fortress.

Nehemiah gets news of the deplorable state of Jerusalem's walls, while he is in Persia serving the emperor as his cupbearer, a high position of trust. Realising his call to spearhead the restoration project, Nehemiah receives permission from the emperor to return to Judah to rebuild its walls.[133] The Jews desperately needed someone who had the vision to restore Jerusalem and Israel to her former glory, someone who was on fire for God and had vision. Nehemiah was God's vessel for such a mandate.

We live in a different time from Nehemiah, but our circumstances today and relationship with God are not very different. We, too, desperately need people with vision for much-needed restoration through divine intervention. Our walls of decency and goodness in society have been torn down and destroyed. It is no longer a secret to most of us that the church in our day is a mere shadow of its former self. The church is no different from the world, for the gates of glory that identified the church as the house of God have been burned by the flames of sin and tarnished by apathy.

Let's look at the steps Nehemiah took in response to all the challenges that faced him. Could this be our strategy to reviving our society?

PRAY A PRAYER OF IDENTIFICATION REPENTANCE

When Nehemiah heard the news about Jerusalem's walls, he wept and mourned for many days, fasting and praying before God.

---

[133] See Nehemiah 2:1-10

First, he called upon the great and awesome God, who keeps covenant and shows mercy to those who love Him and observe His commandments. Then he repented of the sins of the children of Israel as well as the sins of his own house. By identifying with their sin and seeing himself as part of the problem, he was standing in the gap according to 1 Chronicles 7:14. He reminded God of the mutual terms of their covenant in which the people had failed God but God had been faithful. He ended with an earnest appeal to God to be mindful of His promise of restoration and favour:

> *"O Lord, I pray, please let Your ear be attentive to the prayer of Your servant, and to the prayer of Your servants who desire to fear Your name; and let Your servant prosper this day, I pray, and grant him mercy in the sight of this man [the king of Persia]."*

> *Nehemiah 1:1-10*

Surely this is a prayer that would touch the heart of God! We would do well to follow the pattern of this same covenantal prayer when we petition God to restore our broken lives, our family and our nation.

EXAMINE THE CONDITION OF THE PLACE

> *Then I arose in the night, I and a few men with me; I told no one what my God had put in my heart to do at Jerusalem; nor was there any animal with me, except the one on which I rode.*

> *Nehemiah 2:12*

When he arrived in Jerusalem, Nehemiah made a secret inspection of the city walls with just a few men because of his enemies. The mountain of debris was alarming. But this was only the symptom of deeper moral and social decay that Nehemiah was soon to discover: infiltration of foreigners and introduction of pagan ways, unlawful marriages to foreign women, corruption, lawlessness, exploitation of the poor, neglect of the Levites who the community were bound by statute to support.

The core issues we face in our modern society are not much different. I think it is accurate to say that they stem from apathy and indifference. Our secret inspection begins with self. Let us first come into that secret place of the Most High God and ask the Holy Spirit to shine His searchlight into the depths of our heart and ask:

> *Who can understand his errors? Cleanse me from secret faults.*
>
> *Psalm 19:12*

RALLY THE SUPPORT OF LIKE-MINDED PEOPLE

> *Then I said to them, "You see the distress that we are in, how Jerusalem lies waste, and its gates are burned with fire. Come and let us build the wall of Jerusalem, that we may no longer be a reproach." And I told them of the hand of my God which had been good upon me, and also of the king's words that he had spoken to me.*
>
> *So they said, "Let us rise up and build." Then they set their hands to this good work.*
>
> *Nehemiah 2:17-18 (emphasis added)*

Amazingly, the people were of one mind: "Let us arise and build." Representatives from all twelve tribes of Israel got down to the work with the priests leading the way. The time and season had come and God had answered his petition.

I cannot stress enough the spirit of unity that must predominate in any major move of restoration. At first, the laborers were overwhelmed by the mountain of waste that was blocking the gates, but in spite of that they soldiered on. Once we put our minds together to work together, God will be unstoppable!

> *So we built the wall, and the entire wall was joined together up to half its height, for the people had a mind to work.*
>
> *Nehemiah 4:6*

This is the time to rally the support of your family, your community, your church leaders. Our walls and gates are in tatters and we have drifted from the stability, peace and reputation we once enjoyed. We have lost our way. Let us come together in one heart and *rebuild!*

DON'T MIND THE BROKEN AND BURNT STONES

The foreigners looked on and scoffed:

> *"What does this bunch of poor, feeble Jews think they're doing? Do they think they can build the wall in a single day by just offering a few sacrifices? Do they actually think they*

can make something of <u>stones from a rubbish heap</u> – and <u>charred ones</u> at that?"

Nehemiah 4:2 (NLT, emphasis added)

The remarkable thing about God is that He uses whatever is available to fashion it into something wonderful. We saw this in the miracle of the five loaves and two fishes. The prophet Jeremiah also had a vision of a potter remaking a vessel that was flawed. Rather than toss it into the trash, He lovingly reshaped it with his own hands according to what he saw fit.[134]

The walls of our life may seem beyond repair because of all the damage caused by our failures, but give them back to the Potter. He will skilfully remake us into that perfect creation He had originally designed.[135]

UNDERSTAND THE HIDDEN MESSAGES BEHIND THE GATES

The work was apportioned in stretches divided by ten gates along the wall. These gates are very significant in terms of their deeper spiritual meaning because they are milestones in our spiritual journey.

- *Sheep Gate*
  This was where the sheep and lambs were led for sacrifice and they immediately remind us of Jesus, the Lamb of God, who takes away the sins of the world. This speaks of our own salvation and the beginning of our new life in Christ.
- *Fish Gate*
  Our first response to knowing Jesus is to spontaneously share our faith with others. It speaks of evangelism as we heed the call to be "fishers of men"[136].
- *Old Gate*
  This reminds me about God's unchanging truths and the need to come back from straying from the paths of righteousness.

  "Stand in the ways and see,
  And ask for the old paths, where the good way is,

---

[134] See Jeremiah 18:4
[135] See Psalm 139:14
[136] Matthew 4:19

And walk in it;
Then you will find rest for your souls.
But they said, 'We will not walk in it.'"

Jeremiah 6:16

We live in a fluid society where time-honoured traditions like marriage, the family, decency, law and order have been pushed aside by the radical left, who wish to establish their own agendas. Are we going to be taken in by the lie that these are 'progressive developments'? Or are we going to wise up and recognise that this is another grand deception to challenge the old paths established by God. If we eat of the tree of the knowledge of good and evil, we shall surely die.[137]

- *Valley Gate*
Valley type experiences – humbling and painful as they are – are a necessary part of our growth. In fact, we are encouraged by James to consider it all joy when we fall into trials:

....knowing that the testing of your faith produces patience.
But let patience have its perfect work, that you may be perfect
and complete, lacking nothing.

James 1:2-4

Let us draw close to the God of the valley, who will comfort us in our affliction and strengthen us in ways we could never have experienced on the mountain of success.

- *Dung Gate*
This was an unpleasant but absolutely necessary place where all the rubbish was removed. Once we come to repentance, we too must not let all the debris of our life block our walk with God. This is not just bad habits and addictions but also ungodly soul ties which hinder our relationship with Jesus. Sometimes deliverance from evil spirits may be necessary.
Clearing away the rubbish in our lives is never easy but the turnaround from this experience can be seen in the next gate.

---

[137] See Genesis 2:16-17

- *Fountain Gate*
  After the rubbish in our lives is cleared out, the fountain begins to flow freely. This speaks to us of the living waters of the Holy Spirit that cleanse and empower us for our renewed walk.

Jesus said, "Everyone who drinks this water will be thirsty again, but whoever drinks the water I give them will never thirst. Indeed, the water I give them will become in them a spring of water welling up to eternal life."

John 4:13-14 (NIV)

And on the last day of the Feast of Tabernacles, Jesus stood up and shouted: "Let anyone who is thirsty come to me and drink. Whoever believes in me, as Scripture has said, rivers of living water will flow from within them."

John 7:37-38

- *Water Gate*
  The Water Gate is located next to the fountain gate since both relate to the water of the word of God and its cleansing effect.

Christ also loved the church and gave Himself for her, that He might sanctify and cleanse her with the washing of water by the word, that He might present her to Himself a glorious church, not having spot or wrinkle or any such thing, but that she should be holy and without blemish.

Ephesians 5:26-27

Does the word of God still challenge you? Does it still drive you to tears? Does it still stir up righteous indignation? Or has modernity taken over your gospel worldview? Many years ago, when I gave my life to Jesus Christ, whenever I heard Bible-based messages preached, I would cry for the state of my sinfulness in a sinful world, and like the Apostle Paul I would say, "O wretched man that I am! who shall deliver me from the body of this death?"[138]

- *Horse Gate*
  The Horse Gate speaks to us of warfare since horses were used in battle and became a symbol of war. But we must discern

---

[138] Romans 7:24-25 (KJV)

which horse we are relying on. Not the chariots and horses of our own human efforts as in Psalm 20:7. Not the white horse in Revelation, which represents the antichrist and global deception.[139] No, we must keep our eyes fixed on Jesus till He comes, resplendent on a white horse to lead us in battle.

And I saw heaven opened, and behold a white horse; and he that sat upon him was called Faithful and True, and in righteousness he doth judge and make war.

Revelation 19:11 (KJV)

Meanwhile, let us recognise we are engaged in a spiritual battle with demonic spirits and let us make use of the spiritual weapons He has given us.[140]

- *East Gate*
  The eastern gate, also called the *Golden Gate* or *Beautiful Gate*, opens out to the Mount of Olives, and we know that when Jesus returns in His second coming,[141] He will enter the city through this gate:

Afterward he brought me to the gate, even the gate that looketh toward the east: And, behold, the glory of the God of Israel came from the way of the east: and his voice was like a noise of many waters: and the earth shined with his glory.

Ezekiel 43:1 (KJV)

The eastern gate has been shut since AD 1540-41 by order of Suleiman the Magnificent, supposedly to obstruct such an event, but ironically, this fulfils another prophecy by Ezekiel:

Then He brought me back to the outer gate of the sanctuary which faces toward the east, but it was shut. And the LORD said to me, "This gate shall be shut; it shall not be opened, and

---

[139] See Revelation 6:2
[140] See Ephesians 6:11-17
[141] The second coming of Jesus Christ is a fundamental doctrine of the Christian church. It is time of great expectation and the ultimate goal is reflected in the Old Testament (e.g. Zechariah 14:4) and in the New Testament (e.g. Matthew 24:30), as well as in Revelation 1:7.

no man shall enter by it, because the LORD God of Israel has entered by it; therefore it shall be shut.

Ezekiel 44:1-2

- *Inspection Gate*

  The final gate in our Christian journey is the inspection gate. This gate speaks to us of the final judgment of our lives by the Lord at the second coming of Jesus. The ultimate judgment is at the Bema Seat[142] of Christ, where we will have to give an account of our works and be rewarded appropriately:

  For we must all appear before the judgment seat of Christ, that each one may receive the things done in the body, according to what he has done, whether good or bad.

2 Corinthians 10:5

  For the unsaved, there awaits the Great White Throne Judgment[143]. This is the place where every Christ-rejecting soul will be cast into the lake of fire.[144]

ANTICIPATE YOUR ENEMY'S MOVES

Sanballat, Tobiah and Geshem were regional governors serving under the king of Persia. Envious of the restoration project, they used various tactics to disrupt the work and to target Nehemiah himself, seeking to harm him.

---

[142] The word 'judge' is crucial to understanding the two kinds of judgements. Judge as used here serves dual purposes: reward and condemnation. The Scriptures state that those who believe in Jesus Christ will be judged by reward and those that do not believe in Jesus Christ will be judged by condemnation. These two judgments are referred to as the Bema and the Great White Throne Judgement. The Bema Seat (see 2 Corinthians 5:10) is where a believer gives an account of his / her stewardship to Christ. In contemporary terms, it is a tribunal for rewards for successful completion of the race and the place to receive rewards or crowns, but it is important to note that saints will be rewarded accordingly and not equally, as some will suffer loss (see 1 Corinthians 3:15 and 2 John 8).

[143] The Great White Throne Judgement is where those who reject Jesus Christ's offer of salvation during their lifetime will be judged and condemned; see Revelation 20:11-15 and John 5:22,27

[144] See Revelation 20:14

It is interesting to note that at first the enemies mocked and jeered when Nehemiah's motley crew got down to work. But the moment the gaps in the wall had closed – although the wall was only half its height – that was when the enemy really got perturbed and began to launch their attacks.[145]

Let us be encouraged by the fact that our enemies surface when we are doing well and are about to have a breakthrough. So, let's not get sidetracked by them. Many churches face strife and division within the congregation just as God is about to do a mighty work. The main thing is to be aware of Satan's devices and take the necessary countermeasures. It may mean more prayer, corrective action or confronting the dissenting parties in the spirit of love.

And at the individual level, those of us who are facing hardships of various kinds are often taunted by those who say, "Where is your God? What have all your prayers come to?" Let us refuse to give in to the temptation to doubt God but let us hold on to His promises.

ADDRESS THE CRITICAL ISSUES

Nehemiah realised that the broken walls were a symptom of deeper injustices and rifts in his society. He knew that the injustices needed to be resolved in order to rebuild their lives. This would be an ongoing problem, but he and Ezra tackled the most critical issues first.

As we see both in our country and within the church, there is frequent conflict and injustice. The church alone has a remedy, a Person, who can bring peace to any situation. We must bring Him into the picture at every turn. Let us pray and come together in the spirit of unity and examine the deeper roots of all our moral and social issues, singling out the ones that must be given priority.

RENEW OUR COVENANT WITH GOD

On the first day of the seventh month the people gathered at the Water Gate and asked Ezra the priest to read to them the law of Moses, which they had neglected for a long time.

As Ezra reads the law, the people weep.

And Nehemiah, who was the governor, and Ezra the priest and scribe, and the Levites who taught the people said to all

---

[145] See Nehemiah 4:6

the people, "This day is holy to the LORD your God; do not mourn or weep." For all the people wept as they heard the words of the Law.

Nehemiah 8:9 (ESV)

Many of them were learning about their destiny for the first time. It's true that during their exile in Babylon there were no synagogues to preach the word; but had they not been commanded to constantly mediate on and speak the word to their children in their everyday life?[146] In other words, there would be a strong oral tradition to keep that word alive. Sadly, they had failed to do this.

Would you weep, too, when you realise you have been robbed of your heritage and a vital relationship? Would you weep when you know the extent of His longing for you? Is this the legacy we have left our children – a lack of God's word – leaving them in darkness? Are all they have empty platitudes and a form of godliness without the power, leaving them defenceless against the wiles of Satan? This is a strong indictment of our secular culture and lack of parenting.

The reading of the law was the beginning of twenty-four days of both hearing the word read and worshipping the Lord through the week-long Feast of Tabernacles. On the eighth day of Tabernacles the people and their leaders gathered together again and blessed the Lord:

"Stand up and bless the Lord your God from everlasting to everlasting. Blessed be your glorious name, which is exalted above all blessing and praise."

Nehemiah 9:5 (ESV)

Ezra then began his supplication. This was a very intense prayer, which involved all the leaders, spiritual heads, Levites and priests binding their hearts together in agreement before the Lord. They wanted to be free from oppression and slavery – they had seen enough. They had been abandoned for generations as a result of disobedience. Now they were going to re-establish their relationship with God by retracing their paths to Him. It was both a private and corporate matter as they stood and confessed their sins and the iniquities of their fathers; then each leader signed a written agreement to renew his commitment to God.

---

[146] See Deuteronomy 11:19

Because of all this we make a firm covenant in writing; on the sealed document are the names of our princes, our Levites, and our priests.

Nehemiah 9:38 (ESV)

Like the children of Israel who rebuilt the burnt and broken stones of their lives, let us renew our covenant with a faithful and just God. Let us rededicate our personal lives, the lives of our children and our nation to Him. We, too, can experience His blessing, not because we deserve it but because He is a God who honours covenant and shows us His mercies and lovingkindness, especially His never-ending grace.

Contact the Author

To contact the author, please write to:

Michael Angley Ogwuche
c/o Onwards and Upwards Publishers Ltd.
4 The Old Smithy
Rockbeare
EX5 7DX

Or send an email to:

mikeangley@ymail.com

More information about the author can be found
on the book's web page:

www.onwardsandupwards.org/preparing-for-revival

Subscribe to the Author's Podcast

https://www.spreaker.com/user/pneuma
https://podcasts.apple.com/us/podcast/pneuma-podcast/id1454677871

Related Books from the Publisher

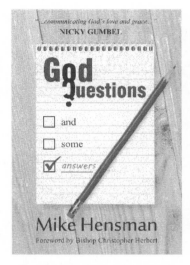

God Questions
Mike Hensman
ISBN 978-1-910197-51-6

In this helpful, easy-to-read guide, Rev. Mike Hensman tackles 46 of the most common questions concerning the Christian faith. With an endorsement from Nicky Gumbel, this is an excellent resource for anyone seeking answers to the important questions of life, as well as those who wish to grow further in their faith.

The Basics of Christianity
John-William Noble
ISBN 978-1-911086-16-1

What does it mean to be a Christian? Why do people get baptised? What is the point of church? Pastor John-William Noble answers these and other common questions about the Christian faith in this helpful interactive guide, useful for small groups or for individual study.

Available from your local Christian bookshop
or direct from the publisher:

www.onwardsandupwards.org